(EXTRA)ORDINARY

INSPIRATIONAL STORIES OF EVERYDAY PEOPLE

KEITH MAGINN

This book is dedicated to those who serve others
and try to make the world a better place,
that they have strength and wisdom;
and to all who are suffering,
that they may find relief.

Contents

Preface

Life is damn hard, way more difficult than I thought it would be. As a kid, I naively thought we grew out of things like anger, jealousy, and heartbreak when we got older. Boy, was I wrong.

People are pretty adept at hiding their issues. To look at Facebook, you'd think everyone is living happy, wonderful lives. And I don't need to tell you about all of the negativity and sensationalism daily in the news.

Sometimes I wish previous generations had done a better job of warning us of how tough things would be. At least then we could have been prepared. Maybe they thought it best we believe in the fairy tale for as long as possible.

While the idea of this book took shape, I saw many people around me struggling in their lives. Divorces, layoffs, addictions, financial stress, depression…on and on. I wanted to highlight feel-good stories to give them hope.

Fortunately, I know several people who are an inspiration to the rest of us. I asked if they would be willing to let me share their stories with anyone who might read this book. These brave souls gave me their time, invited me into their homes, and poured out their hearts. For all of this, I am grateful.

I quote the people in this book fairly often, because hearing directly from the source is important. This gives readers a better idea of the heroes' personalities and captures their feelings in the moments when certain events took place.

Writing this book gave me even more respect for people as a whole. Most of us are doing the best we can with the cards we've been dealt, often in trying circumstances. Thank God we are not in this thing called life on our own. We need one another.

One of the things Dr. Jennifer Rafey and I talked about when I interviewed her for this project was that everyone has a story. And the reality is many people are struggling with something, which brings to mind the wise quote, "Be kinder than necessary, for everyone you meet is fighting some kind of battle."

We are survivors. Often, the periods of adversity are when we find out what we're made of and that we are stronger than we think. We are also reminded about what is important in life.

The people I admire aren't perfect. They are flawed. They are, in a word, human. I can relate to someone like that. We pull for the underdog, and every so often, the underdog prevails against all odds.

Most of us face struggles we have to overcome. We either can give up or we can keep giving our best effort. With this in mind, the stories in this book are about people I know who have gone through significant challenges. Their wills were tested, or they took a leap of faith.

So here's to family, friends, coworkers…to parents, like you'll meet in this book, who are willing to do anything for their children…to those trying to live life to the fullest…to those who help others along the way. May God bless you all. I hope these stories inspire you as much as they have inspired me.

Keith Maginn

Summer 2016

Cincinnati, Ohio, USA

Curt (part one)

Black-haired and mustached 39-year-old Curt Schaeffer arrived at his gate at Juan Santamaria International Airport around 5:15 a.m. on October 21, 1989. Though based in New York, he was visiting local offices as the Deputy Regional Manager for Latin American operations for CARE, an international relief and development non-profit organization. For the past week, he had been working at the CARE office in San Jose, Costa Rica. His wife, Magaly (pronounced "Muh-GOL-ly"), was meeting Curt later that morning in Tegucigalpa, Honduras, where the couple planned to celebrate Magaly's birthday together a day late.

Curt was anxious about flying with a non-U.S. carrier, but no American airlines were available in that region. One of only 138 passengers on the Boeing 727-200, Curt was going to sit in the back of the plane before a flight attendant suggested he might prefer a more comfortable, unoccupied first-class seat near the front. Curt settled his slender, 6-foot-2 body into a fourth-row aisle seat on the aircraft's right side.

The passengers had a short, smooth trip to a stopover at Augusto C. Sandino Airport in Managua, Nicaragua. After a brief respite to board several more passengers,

Flight Number 414 resumed. The 30-minute haul would get passengers to Tegucigalpa at 8 a.m.

As the plane ascended, Curt noticed the weather conditions quickly turning ominous with strong winds and dense clouds. Just as a flight attendant announced they were preparing to land, Curt saw a flash of green out of the corner of his eye. A passenger in front of him shrieked: "No, no, no! We're going to hit!"

In *Escape with One's Life: Learning to Live with Survival,* Curt describes what happened next:

> The impact was immediate as the 170,000-pound behemoth careened across mountainous terrain at an approach speed of close to two hundred miles per hour. We were thrown into darkness. I heard the grotesque sound of metal scraping on earth while people screamed hysterically. My first and only thought was that this was it. I was surely going to die.
>
> I put my arms over my head as I was thrown forward. In a matter of seconds, I passed through a wall of flames. I covered my face with my hands to protect it from the intense heat. There was a dream-like quality to those seconds; I was aware of moving and burning, with no discomfort or any control over what was happening. I lost consciousness.
>
> I came to in a field. I was still belted into my seat. Miraculously, I was sitting upright as I had been

inside the plane. My aisle seat had separated from the window seat next to me, and I was ejected from the plane. A short distance to my right was the blazing inferno of the exploding 727. High winds whipped the flames away from me.

I felt numb. I looked down at my hands and arms and noticed a pale, lifeless quality. The skin had been burned. I was still in a stunned state but was regaining my senses. I seemed to be the only one in this field—no other survivors, no dead people, no locals, nobody else but me! The odd sight momentarily struck me as being surreal until I felt chills course through my body.

I was in a state of shock, and it did not occur to me to try to rescue other passengers, as the plane was an inferno. I assumed that they had escaped on the other side of the fuselage.

Curt was doused in fuel oil, his left shoe missing. Cold and in pain, he was able to unbuckle his seatbelt and stand up. He then stumbled to a small house a few hundred yards below him while coughing up smoke from his lungs. A woman in the house—no doubt startled at the intrusion of a disheveled foreigner—offered him water, but Curt declined when he noticed the water was dirty.

Stepping outside, he saw other survivors who had staggered or were carried from the wreckage getting into a small pickup truck on the dirt road. Without a word, Curt climbed into the truck bed. Two men in bad condition were lying on their backs. While the truck owner's young daughter gazed wide-eyed at the bewildered group, her father drove them an hour to the Hospital Escuela in Tegucigalpa.

"Those of us who survived were struggling with the shock of our own survival—second- and third-degree burns, multiple fractures, and the terror of what we had just experienced," Curt says. "We were quickly becoming aware of the fact that survival has both physical and emotional costs."

Curt was extremely fortunate to survive the tragedy on the mountainside (named Cerro de Hula), but the road ahead would be far from easy. Physically, he would have to endure grueling measures to repair the burns on his body; mentally, Curt would be terrorized by sadness, anger, and nightmares of the awful scene he had narrowly escaped.

He would also face another major ordeal: guilt over having survived when others did not. Of the 138 passengers on Flight 414, Curt was one of 11 survivors. Four of the eight crew members lost their lives. In total, 15 had made it; 131 had not.

Some died on impact, but many were burned alive. Most of the victims were Hondurans and Nicaraguans. Ten Americans were killed. Because authorities were slow to cordon off the area, looters had ransacked the debris. Valuables were stolen from corpses, including wallets and jewelry. (Some locals later were arrested and charged with theft.)

The disaster devastated Honduras and neighboring Nicaragua, homes to 104 of the deceased passengers. Three days of national mourning were declared. U.S. President George H. W. Bush and Pope John Paul II were among those who sent their condolences.

Why had the flight attendant recommended Curt move to a seat at the front of the aircraft, which probably saved his life? (Ten of the survivors were in the front of the cabin, four in the middle, and one at the rear. Curt had been heading to the back.) Why was Curt's seat ejected, and how did he land upright in a field, far enough away to avoid the explosion? Why didn't he burn up like so many other passengers, even though he was covered in fuel oil?

Curt reasoned:

> It is a miracle that there were any survivors at all. The plane flew out of a cloud right into the mountainside. One possible mitigating factor was that the pilots did have a few seconds to try to pull the plane back up into the air and, in so doing, caused the nose to break off. Most of the survivors were sitting in the front of the plane. It was propitious, too, that the aircraft made impact on a small but relatively flat soccer field and not on the rougher terrain of the surrounding mountainside.

Two months shy of 40 years old, Curt Schaeffer was one of the few to live through the worst air catastrophe in the history of Central America.

Dr. Jennifer

"I come from a very close-knit family," says Dr. Jennifer Rafey. Her father got sick with non-Hodgkin lymphoma when his daughter was around 10 years old, and he died when she was 12, her brothers 9 and 4. Dr. Jennifer's father was only 38 years old.

Dr. Jennifer saw the slow process of her father dying in front of his young family. She remembers him getting sick while lying on the couch, looking green, and losing his hair. But she didn't fully comprehend the finality of his death.

The loss was devastating but made the young siblings closer. "We didn't fight, none of that," Dr. Jennifer states. "It made us much tighter, absolutely."

She continues:

"My mother, a widow at 36, raised my two brothers and me. We spent a lot of time together, and my mom never let me forget the importance of knowing who you are and where you come from. I took that philosophy with me as I became a parent."

Life after her father's death was a huge transition. Her grandparents stepped in more in an attempt to keep things "normal." Much of Dr. Jennifer's heartache came in seeing her mom's sadness. She says her mother remained heart-broken until the day she died.

Though Dr. Jennifer's father had been a prominent engineer with about a dozen patents to his name, Dr. Jennifer's parents didn't have any life-insurance money set aside, due to pre-existing health conditions. Her mother had been a stay-at-home mom before Dr. Jennifer's dad passed away. After his death, her mother's previous employer offered her mom big money at a corporate job, but she turned down the position. Instead, she earned a master's degree and became a teacher in order to be home with her children in the summertime.

She somehow raised three kids in the same house they lived in when their dad died and sent them to private schools. Her mom tried to fill the roles of both mom and dad, good and bad cop. "How she did all of that," Dr. Jennifer says, shaking her head, "I have no idea."

Dr. Jennifer was a cheerleader and played soccer as a youth. She was involved with her church and was on the dance team at Alter High School in Kettering, Ohio. Dr. Jennifer also babysat "a ton" and worked alongside one of her brothers at Taco Bell. While earning a bachelor's degree in environmental health science and graduating summa cum laude from Wright State University near Dayton, Ohio, she worked at Lane Bryant.

She'd always wanted to help people live more healthful lives, and she originally thought about being a pediatrician. While she was in college, a family friend was looking for help in his chiropractic office a few days a week. Dr. Jennifer worked directly with patients for two years and saw many of their lives transformed. "People who had been everywhere came in without hope, unable to move," she says, "but finally got the care and attention they needed and deserved."

The chiropractor, whom Dr. Jennifer describes as "brilliant," willingly worked with other health professionals to get patients what they needed. Dr. Jennifer appreciated his approach and witnessed the lives he changed. She also realized her calling was to be a chiropractor.

Unfortunately, tragedy struck her family again. On June 9, 1999, her mother was diagnosed with breast cancer. Dr. Jennifer bounced back and forth between Logan College of Chiropractic in St. Louis, Missouri, and home to help with her mother's care. Nonetheless, Dr. Jennifer received top honors at Logan in 2001, while nannying on the side. Dr. Jennifer's work ethic and success should come as no shock. Considering her mom's approach to life, "we were going to college, no doubt about it."

Though she had been given two years to live, Dr. Jennifer's mom survived more than seven. She fought until the end, including her last three weeks in hospice care without any food or water. "She wasn't afraid to die," Dr. Jennifer clarifies. "She was afraid to leave my brothers and me."

Her mom passed away on November 3, 2006. The number of visitors for Dr. Jennifer's mother astounded the hospice workers, who asked, "What did she do?" They'd never seen so many people come to pay their respects. Former students, colleagues, family, and friends came in droves from all over. "It was packed," says Dr. Jennifer, smiling.

Twenty years after losing her father, Dr. Jennifer, 32 years old, and her brothers, 29 and 24, were now parentless. Dealing with her mother's death was even tougher than losing her father, because Dr. Jennifer was an adult and therefore more aware of her mother's suffering. After all, she had been so young when her father passed that she didn't know much of her childhood any other way.

Instead of wilting under the hurt, the resilient and vivacious Dr. Jennifer continued to flourish. She and her then-husband opened Rafey Chiropractic and Health Center. With her light brown, shoulder-length hair, and smart, down-to-earth personality, Dr. Jennifer could have been one of the lead female roles on the hit TV show *Friends* if she'd been an actress instead of a chiropractor.

Primarily, she loves adjusting patients, which Dr. Jennifer believes is a gift that makes her unique and enables patients to find healing after first having searched many other places: "Most of all, I love the words of gratitude, hugs, and kind notes. I love knowing that I am making the lives I touch daily a little bit better."

An outstanding chiropractor, Dr. Jennifer is a mother first and foremost. She has five children—four daughters and one son—ranging from high school age to kindergarten. Dr. Jennifer is involved in many of their school, church, and extracurricular activities.

"They are my everything," she says, beaming. "My world begins and ends with them. I work hard every day to instill in them the values and relationships that my mother taught me."

Dr. Jennifer tries to lead her family by example, believing actions speak louder than words. "Sometimes it can be a balancing act between a full-time practice and a mother of five," she says. "As I see my children grow and change every day, I know that every ounce of effort is worth it."

Dr. Jennifer enjoys being with family and friends, going to movies, and reading books when not treating patients or acting as maid and chauffeur to her kids. "I love to cook—not bake!—and love, love, *love* to travel," she says. She tries to find time for doing home renovations, decorating, and spending time outdoors, especially hiking and boating.

Dr. Jennifer lives by three principles that she tries to instill in her children. First: *What you think about, you bring about.*

"Fill your mind and interactions with positivity and positive experiences—friendships, shows, music, etc. All of it factors in. If you think bad things will happen, they will; if you think good things will come, they will."

Second: *Be the change you wish to see in the world.*

"The world is filled with so much in need of change. I truly believe the change is going to come from small, random acts of kindness. If we treat others in a manner that will better the world, then positive change will come. Often people really need a held door, kind word, or listening ear. A smile can change a person's life."

Third: *Little hinges swing big doors.*

"It doesn't take a very big hinge to swing a massive door. The smallest act, thought, or change can make all the difference. If you want to make a change for the better, you may just need to change one small aspect of your life."

Despite losing both of her parents when she was fairly young, in many ways her divorce was Dr. Jennifer's toughest test and life-changer. Though Dr. Jennifer and her husband separated in 2012 and divorced in 2014, they continued working together and have a good relationship. Dr. Jennifer's ex-husband left the practice in June 2014 to pursue other professional opportunities, and Dr. Jennifer now owns and runs the Colerain location on her own.

When the couple initially parted ways, Dr. Jennifer's life turned upside down. Formerly, Dr. Jennifer had been predominantly a stay-at-home mom. Suddenly, she had more roles to fill at a busy practice, not to mention becoming the main caretaker of five children.

Balancing home and work is her primary challenge. Dr. Jennifer regrets she can't be as much of a mother as she'd like. She wants to do more "mom stuff" but is pulled in many different directions. "I didn't have a choice," she says. "I had five kids to care for. And here we go!"

Being raised by a single mother gave her confidence that she, like her mom, could make things work. Recalling how she and her brothers were cared for gave her an "OK, I can do this" mindset. Again like her mother, she doesn't see herself as strong, even though everyone else does.

The divorce was a loss and her new responsibilities are demanding, but Dr. Jennifer is not bitter. The silver lining is she was thrust into the role of direct patient care, which she loves. Whereas before she had been more behind the scenes at Rafey Chiro and her then-husband had done nearly all of the adjusting, Dr. Jennifer moved into full-time adjusting after his departure, which would not have happened otherwise.

I have been a loyal patient of Dr. Jennifer's for several months. I heard about Rafey Chiropractic through a friend whose insomnia and migraines disappeared after going to Rafey on her friend's recommendation. I had been thinking about going to a chiropractor and decided to check out Rafey Chiro—a 30-minute drive one way for me—instead of many closer locations due to my friend's ringing endorsement. This turned out to be a wise decision.

After getting a thorough patient history, Dr. Jennifer came up with a specific treatment plan for me. Admittedly, I am not the usual patient. My health situation is…complex. In addition to living with chronic back pain for more than 20 years, I had trouble with my feet, calves, knees, pelvis, and hips. In the past three years, I'd had five surgeries. Physically, I was an absolute mess.

I knew I'd require several visits to see positive results, but I expressed my reservations about an extended regimen. My health-care plan allotted only 15 covered visits. Anything further would be coming out of my pocket.

In addition, I'd taken a leap of faith and left my full-time job to focus on my health, promoting my first two books, and writing the book you are now reading. After depleting my checking and savings accounts, I was living off my early-withdrawn retirement savings. Money was tight, as in, "How in the world am I ever going to afford this?"

Aware of my concerns, Dr. Jennifer didn't blink an eye. She said getting me healthy was the most important thing; we would make things work financially. Her kindness and unselfishness meant a lot to me.

When I'd exhausted my 15 covered visits, Dr. Jennifer contacted my health insurance provider to request supplementary visits on my behalf. She made clear that more appointments were necessary and would be of great benefit to my health for years to come, which would help both me and my provider. Request denied.

Undeterred, Dr. Jennifer said my continued visits were imperative because we were seeing results, so she and I would barter. She needed help updating her website and wanted a professional-looking biography she could use at conferences, for fliers, and for social media. I could help her with these and others tasks she would come up with down the road, and we would continue my treatment at a reduced, much more affordable rate. (Can you imagine a typical Western doctor doing this for a patient? Me neither.)

Dr. Jennifer was adamant I get massage therapy, as well. I wondered how I could afford this additional service, and she said not to worry. She paired me with one of her three on-site massage therapists, Kelly Myers, who Dr. Jennifer thought would be the best match for my needs. After several weeks of massages, Kelly and Dr. Jennifer agreed I needed longer sessions, so they bumped me up from 30 to 60 minutes.

However, Rafey Chiropractic wouldn't raise my rate a cent. Dr. Jennifer cited my book *Goodwill Tour: Paying It Forward* and said she would happily pay it forward to me, "a good person trying to do good things." Again, my health and well-being were her focus, not the almighty dollar. (Kelly essentially gives me the additional half-hour at no cost to me, for which I am eternally grateful, as she could easily fill my time slot with a full-paying customer.)

Though touched by the big hearts of Dr. Jennifer and Kelly, I wasn't surprised. Dr. Jennifer has surrounded herself with an awesome staff. Rafey Chiropractic is popular and can get quite busy—she averages around 250 visits a week—but Dr. Jennifer and her staff remain calm and friendly at all times. They are a pleasure to be around. The Rafey Chiro family is a positive, caring group from the top down.

When asked about the wonderful team she has built, Dr. Jennifer says they are people she already knew or they were referred by someone she trusted. "I go a lot on intuition," Dr. Jennifer admits. "You can teach people procedures, but there are certain qualities that you can't teach people, like caring and being genuine. So these are the main things I look for."

As a result, Dr. Jennifer's patients love her and her outgoing and encouraging team. Many patients find Dr. Jennifer's mind-and-body approach refreshing. Dr. Jennifer explains:

"Yeah, it's a job, but I see it more as a gift. So many people don't have access to quality health care. I often don't know their financial or insurance situation, so it doesn't change how I treat them. I'm not looking at people as a number. I strive to offer every single patient the care that I would expect for myself and my family—I won't settle for less, and I don't think my patients should either. I give to them selflessly, but they all give more to me in return than they will ever know."

After several twice-a-week visits, Dr. Jennifer and I developed a healthy doctor/patient relationship. To this day, we joke around and compare how many times we continue to leave our vehicles' sunroofs open overnight. I ask about her kids and she gives me dating advice, always "keeping an eye out for the perfect girl" for me.

Dr. Jennifer is wholeheartedly dedicated to her patients' entire health—meaning body, mind, and soul—and does everything she can for us. Dr. Jennifer is the kind of boss who posts on Facebook about how amazing her staff is, thanks them, and tells them she loves them. She balances being a boss, a friend, and a role model effortlessly.

When asked how she handles running a business, caring for numerous patients, and being a great mother of five, Dr. Jennifer bursts out laughing, "Organized chaos!" Characteristically, she then sends the credit to others:

"I have the best support in the world—two great babysitters, my brothers, sisters-in-law, and Dave [her boyfriend, 'a great guy who the kids just love']. I couldn't do it without a village. And I don't sweat the small stuff—we eat on paper plates sometimes."

Understandably, she still misses her parents. "It's not just the holidays," she says, sighing. "It's the little things, like seeing families with multiple generations out to eat together."

After her mother's funeral, Dr. Jennifer stopped by the house of her mom's close friend, where the entire family was eating "a Norman Rockwell dinner." When Dr. Jennifer walked to her car after visiting, the truth sunk in: "Oh my gosh, I have no home. There is no more going home."

Dr. Jennifer is quick to mention that her mom was a great example and provided well—she owned her house and car and owed nothing when she died. She always found a way to take her kids on a vacation each summer. Her mother also stressed the importance of immediate and extended family, which stuck with her daughter.

Dr. Jennifer tries to go the extra mile because her kids don't have her parents as grandparents. She makes time for herself a priority occasionally, recalling how her mom was a "mother only" who didn't do anything just for herself.

Dr. Jennifer's vibrant chiropractic practice continues to help her community. She is currently working to incorporate more health care providers on site to offer even more complete mind, body, and soul treatment for her patients.

As usual, her five kids keep her constantly on the go, and she smiles through it all. In late 2014, *Cincy Magazine* listed Dr. Jennifer as one of the top chiropractors in the Cincinnati area as rated by her peers.

Wise beyond her years, Dr. Jennifer is well aware we never know what life has in store for us. "Embrace the path God gives you," she advises. "All the things I've been through, positive or negative, made me more compassionate and made me who I am." Losing her parents was difficult, but the experiences became building blocks that empowered her to handle life's challenges.

All you need to know to understand Dr. Jennifer Rafey is her main ambition in life:

"When I lay on my death bed, I look in my children's eyes and they know that I loved them and that I helped them become wonderful, loving, kind adults. That right there is my life's work; nothing else really matters. I want to help make this world a better place, and I want it to start with me and my family."

....

If you would like to make a donation in honor of Dr. Jennifer Rafey, she asks that you donate "time, talent, or treasure" wherever you think it will make a difference.

Matt, Kaytee, and Jack

Matt Roettgers has more nicknames than anyone else I have ever met: Roe (rhymes with "Joe"), Roe Dog, Roe Diggity, Roach, Roach Cakes, Cupcakes, Little Roe Sheep, Rohann Sebastian Bach, the Notorious R.O.E.…the list goes on.

Roe and I met in 1997, my freshman and his sophomore year at Miami University. Matt and I lived at the Evans Scholars House with about 40 other former caddies for three of our four college years. (All of us had earned a scholarship for golf caddying, good grades, and community service… no joke!)

Matt is also from Cincinnati, where he went to Purcell Marian High School, the high school both of our dads attended. Roe and I clicked instantly at the Evans House, realizing we share a love of sports, beer, and music, especially Dave Matthews Band and Bob Marley. Matt is a fun-loving, hilarious, and laid-back redhead.

Matt and I had a lot of fun together at Miami. One of my favorite Roe stories is from New Year's Eve several years ago. Because Roe and I were both single among a group of couples, he leaned over at midnight without warning and kissed me right on the lips.

I was not expecting that.

In the summer of 2006, Matt and his teammates would meet after games at the bar that sponsored their softball team. Kaytee (like "Katie") Gantzer, with sandy blonde hair, blue eyes, a small nose ring, and a quick wit, bartended there at the time. When several weeks of her obvious flirting went unacknowledged by Roe, Kaytee followed him to his car one night for a goodbye hug: "Luckily it was a really dark bar, so I guess that is why she liked me so much." Dark bar or not, Matt finally realized Kaytee was after him.

The two began dating on June 17, 2006, and married in August 2009. They had an outdoor wedding, followed by a reception complete with a reggae band: "We still go to weddings where people come up to us and say that we had one of the best receptions ever." (I was honored to be one of the groomsmen, and I can attest to the greatness of the reception.)

In April 2011, Kaytee found out she was two months pregnant. They had an earlier-than-usual ultrasound in June at 19 weeks so they could discover the gender of the baby. Matt and Kaytee brought champagne bottles with them to their Saturday morning appointment, along with "It's a Boy!" and "It's a Girl!" stickers.

They requested the technician put the appropriate sticker on the bottles without telling them and then zip the bottles up in a soft-sided cooler. At a pool party at their house later that afternoon, Matt and Kaytee reached into the cooler to find out the gender of their child in front of family and friends. When they pulled out "It's a Boy!" bottles, Roe was so excited he did a cannonball into the pool.

Their joy didn't last long.

Matt explains: "We couldn't have been more excited. We were having a 'Jack.' But a week later, excitement turned into anxiety—Jack had CDH."

At their more in-depth 20-week ultrasound, Roe and Kaytee were told Jack had Congenital Diaphragmatic Hernia. CDH is a condition in which a hole in the diaphragm allows the intestines and other organs to move into the chest, which restricts the development of the lungs. This can cause reduced blood flow to the lungs and pulmonary hypertension (high blood pressure).

CDH occurs in one of every 2,500 births and is life-threatening if untreated. There are 1,600 cases in the United States per year. The cause of CDH is unknown. Only 50 percent of live CDH births will survive.

After so much initial excitement, things looked grim. In fact, Jack's lungs were undetectable on the MRI. Kaytee said Jack's intestines looked like millions of worms taking over her unborn son's chest.

Understandably, Matt and Kaytee were struck with doubt and depression. Doctors suggested termination or comfort care—a program for care of children with life-threatening conditions, focusing on enhancing the quality of life for as long as possible and minimizing suffering for the child and family—as possible options. Kaytee says they didn't flinch:

"Matt and I could not understand having to make a decision of life or slow death. We faced forward and counted the days until Jack's birth."

They supported each other and prayed a lot. Kaytee thought about scouring the Internet for CDH success stories, but she feared coming across accounts that did not have a happy ending.

On September 5, 2011, Kaytee's water broke, just 29 weeks into the pregnancy. Doctors said her going into labor at 35 weeks or less would give Jack even less than a one-in-five chance, reducing his odds of survival from 50 percent to 20 percent. Again, hospital personnel suggested comfort care as an option. Matt and Kaytee would have none of it. Kaytee would have to give birth at this stage anyway, so they figured they should give Jack a chance. As Roe said later, "We were signed on no matter what; after all, 20 percent is not 0 percent."

Kaytee was put on bed rest at Good Samaritan Hospital, near the University of Cincinnati. She would be exclusively bedridden, save for bathroom trips and twice-weekly ultrasounds. Rest for the mother and weight gain for the fetus would be the most important factors for the baby's survival. The goal was to get Kaytee to the 38-week mark, making her full-term.

After nine weeks in bed at Good Sam, Kaytee and Jack made it to 38 weeks. The night before the scheduled delivery, Kaytee was scared and asked Matt to hold her. He climbed into the hospital bed and listened to her concerns.

Kaytee asked her husband for one favor:

"The only request I had for Matt is that if Jack wouldn't make it and I was still under general anesthesia, I wanted Matt to tell Jack that I love him and I tried my hardest. Matt accepted my request but assured me that he would not have to repeat those words and that I would be able to tell Jack 'I love you' myself."

At 3 a.m. on November 7, Kaytee was transferred from Good Samaritan to Cincinnati Children's Hospital Medical Center by non-emergency ambulance for the delivery. Around 40 people, all with different specialties and responsibilities, would be helping with the birth. The fate of the Roettgers family was now in the hands of the hospital staff.

Matt wishes he could say the day of the birth was exciting, but it was mostly worrisome. He wasn't permitted in the delivery room, due to space limitations. He was told to put on teal scrubs, later learning this was in case something went wrong and he was the lone parent available to say goodbye to Jack.

At 7 a.m., Kaytee was taken to the operating table, and the ensuing few hours were a blur. The delivery was supposed to take two to three hours but lasted closer to five. The doctors had planned to deliver Jack partially and then hook him up to a heart and lung bypass machine, called Extracorporeal Membrane Oxygenation (ECMO). The machine would breathe and pump blood for him, because Jack couldn't yet do so on his own. (Most of the CDH patients who don't survive are lost during this phase.)

But there were complications and the doctor decided to cut the umbilical cord before Jack was on ECMO. If he did not cut the cord, there was a chance of losing both Kaytee and Jack; if he did, then Mom would be safe and they would hope for the best for the baby.

The decision worked.

Kaytee woke up crying in agony hours later. She was in and out of consciousness. One minute, Matt and hospital staff surrounded her bed; the next, they were gone. Finally, a nurse came in and said Jack was coming down the hall.

Kaytee reflects:

"He was covered in tubes and not making any movement. He was intubated, covered with IVs and heavily sedated. And beautiful. There we were. Mother and son. Laying feet away from each other and all I wanted to do was kiss his forehead. I asked a nurse if he was OK. I remember her response well. 'He's doing OK.' It was like a symphony to me. My pain was gone for just one moment. Jack was OK. We could move forward. The hurdle that I had been dreading for months was past us. We could now approach the next hurdle.

"I passed out from narcotics at this time. My epidural had worn off shortly after surgery and the anesthesiologist was called to another surgery, so I didn't have any pain medication on board. When the pain team joined me in recovery after about 10 minutes of feeling full pain, I was overloaded with morphine to chase the pain."

Kaytee woke up on the seventh floor of the hospital; Jack was on the third, still fighting for his life. Family surrounded Kaytee and listened as she described her new baby boy as "the most beautiful thing she had ever seen," though she knew he might appear to others as "a tired, old man."

As the hours passed by, Matt was proven right. Jack survived the night and Kaytee was able to tell her son she loved him in person. She knew God was watching over them.

But Jack still had a long way to go. He would remain on ECMO for 15 days, an extremely stressful and scary period for his parents. They were in a holding pattern, unable to move forward until Jack was able to exchange gases on his own.

"He was still on a ventilator, which did the actual mechanical breathing for him. He just had to be able to exchange carbon dioxide for oxygen," Kaytee says. "What presented the challenge is that he didn't have that much lung tissue (and was actually undetected on MRI at this point)."

The doctors watched Jack closely, trying to decide when to take him off of the machine. The decision was a delicate one, as Jack was still quite sick. They did not want him to come off ECMO too soon, nor be hooked to the machine for too long. The waiting game was laborious for Matt and Kaytee—"constant ups and downs for more than two weeks"—until the doctors believed Jack was ready.

Kaytee recounts what happened next:

"November 22, 2011, will be a day that Matt and I will never forget. It was the day we were told to say goodbye to our dying son.

"Two days previous, I was sitting at Jack's bedside; the last bed in a room which resembled army barracks after a midnight surprise attack. Two long rows of isolated cribs positioned side by side, holding babies who were at any stage between healing and dying. I was still on maternity leave from work and spending my entire days next to Jack. Between Jack's impromptu naps, we would talk, read books, and smile at each other. And I would pray for good updates as I waited for daily rounds.

"Dr. L and Dr. F approached the bed space with their team of fellows, specialists, nurses, and residents. They started talking about Jack's progress; he was improving every day and was healing well after his CDH repair surgery. Besides the fact that his ECMO circuit had a number of replacement membranes, his biometrics showed that he was ready to come off ECMO and breathe only with the assistance of a ventilator.

"After rounds were completed, the doctors moved on to the next bedside and left Dr. L and Dr. F to further explain their plan. They planned to take Jack off the ECMO circuit and allow his lungs to exchange gases on their own. A review of the benefits and risks was presented, and releases for medical treatment were signed. I was so excited for the progress of my baby's health and quickly called Matt and then the rest of the family. I was bursting at the idea of Jack getting well and someday breaking out of his medical prison.

"There wasn't much for us to do in the way of preparation apart from finding emotional readiness. This was the next step in Jack's journey and it was a do-or-die step. This was the *only* next step.

"The morning of the procedure came early. Surgery on these fragile kiddos takes place in the NICU [Neonatal Intensive Care Unit] right there in the bed space, and all visitors are asked to leave the pod so the area can be sterilized. Matt and I would have to make our way into the pod to say our good mornings and give our kisses before they could start to ready the area for the 7 a.m. start time. We were told that Jack would be mostly sedated with Midazolam (aka Versed) by the time we arrived in the morning. This, however, was not the case. He was wild and kicking off nurses. At first, I was concerned, but Dr. L assured me that this attitude and strength would come in handy when it was time to heal. Matt and I gave Jack our kisses, told him we would be back in when he woke up, and finished some last-minute details with the doctors. Then we were banished to the waiting room.

"The waiting room was half filled with our family and supporters who would spend the next two hours distracting us, and doing a great job at it, too. Occasionally a nurse would come out and give us a report that Jack is doing great and they should be completed soon. Finally, after two hours, the advanced practice nurse came into the waiting room and told us that the procedure was a success and Jack was off ECMO. They were closing him up and would need a couple of minutes to finish up and move the circuit out of the bed space.

"I couldn't believe it. I knew the intended result of the procedure was to take Jack off ECMO, but I was completely amazed that it had finally happened. Looking at that massive machine for 15 days was so de-humanizing and intimidating. And now it was gone.

"For the next hour, we sat in the waiting room with anxiety. Evidently, moving the circuit was a little more involved than I thought. But we were soon granted entry back into the pod and were able to see Jack.

"When we approached the bedside, I was overjoyed and destroyed. There was no goliath of machines looming over my baby's body. The space was clean and free from obstacles. But Jack didn't look like the baby I kissed that morning. He was skinny after the circuit took with it all his extra fluid. It exposed his real weight, which was far from ideal at only a little over 5 pounds but with 20 inches of length. With the lost body mass, the surgical silo holding his intestines outside his abdomen looked large and obtrusive. And his skin had a yellow color; not a glow and not jaundice, but a look of sickness. Something I can't quite explain. But the monitors next to his bed said they were breathing for him and he was exchanging his own gases. The procedure was a success. I cried on Matt's shoulder.

"After a long visit with the new Jack and a complete breakdown of events from the nurses and doctors, Matt and I headed out. Matt had to go in to work, and I was in much need of a shower. I planned to return after my shower and wait for Matt to complete his partial work day.

"Weeks of NICU visits at this point had trained me to look the length of the pod to Jack's bed space before I entered. I wanted that little bit of warning in case something was happening. When I arrived back at the NICU, this was no exception and I scanned to the end of the pod. I could see a collection of doctors and nurses, all still in their green surgery scrubs, standing around the head of Jack's bed. Dr. L stood under the monitors, staring up in contemplation. When I approached the bedside, Dr. L explained to me that after only a couple of hours after the procedure, Jack started to hold his breath and was having trouble exchanging his gases. He was fighting the ventilator though he was still under the control of Midazolam. The carbon dioxide was collecting in his blood and caused it to become acidic. The CO_2 results of his blood gases continued to climb. If he continued this path, even for only a couple more hours, his organs would start to fail, one by one, until he died.

"I begged that he do anything in his power to stop this and quickly left the NICU to pick Matt up from work.

"On our return, the nurses and doctors were where I had left them and there was a little more panic in their faces as we approached the bed space. Dr. L told us that Jack's CO2 was so high, it was no longer being measured by a numerical value. Just a 'more than' on a monitor. He asked us to sit down so we could talk. He said that Jack only had about 30 minutes left. They were doing all they could but hadn't found what changes needed to be made to lower his CO2. They would continue to work until they found a solution or until the end, and suggested that we should go sit with Jack. I felt like I lost all control. I couldn't breathe and doubled over in my seat, hysterical. Someone handed me a trash can and I started to heave with my head half in my basket, crying inaudible words. This is when we met Nurse B.

"Nurse B had signed up to be Jack's primary day nurse and started on the day that he was coming off ECMO. She walked up to me with a box of tissues and assisted me in moving the chair over to Jack's side so I could hold his hand. She told me to tell him that I loved him and that I should be with him if he passes. Matt came to stand beside me and we held Jack's tiny hand. I told Nurse B that Jack knows that I love him and I won't say goodbye to a baby who has to be OK.

"The monitors started to beep louder and more consistently. His heart rate was dropping and his respirations were down to about 6-10 a minute. The monitors were broadcasting that my baby was dying. I said a small prayer as doubt and fear crept into my head but kept hold of his little hand and told him that he would be fine. He could beat this.

"I assume in a move of desperation, Dr. L demanded that the respiratory therapist change the setting on his ventilator. It was a lower setting which would control his breaths a little less and could possibly stop the little breathing that Jack was doing, but it was the only thing that hadn't been tried. The settings were changed and the doctors and nurses stood still, watching the monitors and waiting. After only minutes, the monitors started to slow the alarms. Jack's heart rate began to rise and he started breathing a little more frequently. His little fingers and toes started to twitch a little. There was such a feeling of slight relief that you could feel the air getting cooler and lighter. Over the course of the next hour, Jack's CO_2 had dropped to a level that was measurable. Though this was still a critical point, he was moving in the right direction.

"Matt and I stayed with Jack until late that evening when the nurses finally kicked us out to return home for some sleep. Jack's CO_2 continued to drop throughout the night and into the morning. And you know me, I called several times in the middle of the night because I knew that they would be taking hourly blood gas checks until it reached safe levels. Dr. L even answered my calls a couple of times that night to give me the results himself. What a dedicated life saver!"

Jack would require about a dozen procedures in his first four and a half months of life, including seven surgeries, but he had survived.

Matt, an art director at an advertising company, had to return to work one and a half weeks after Jack's birth. He went to the hospital from work every night. Often, he visited before work or on his lunch break, as well.

Including recovery time post-delivery, Kaytee had been in the hospital for nine weeks and five days. She returned to her job as a research-and-development food scientist five weeks later. There was nothing they could really do at the hospital, so letting work keep them busy and take their minds off things was best. Plus, Jack had some of the preeminent babysitters in the world at the Neonatal Intensive Care Unit at Cincinnati Children's Hospital.

After spending 136 days in the NICU, Jack was released from the hospital. Due to the 11 medications Jack had to take spread out over 24 hours, Roe and Kaytee rarely got more than three to four hours of sleep at a time. The doctors put Jack on methadone to wean him off morphine.

On April 10, 2012, Matt and Kaytee set up a blog (weknowjackdotme.wordpress.com) to keep family and friends updated on Jack's "struggles and achievements with CDH." Kaytee added that they "want Jack's story to give another mom comfort, another dad confidence, and to add another inspiring story to this frightening sea of research, definitions, and anecdotes."

Their own words from the "About Us" section of their blog:

> The Roettgers Family is a unit of four. Matt is a
> graphic artist and a dad; Kaytee is a food scientist

and a mom; Amber is a lovable brown dog; and Jack…he's our miracle. Jack was diagnosed with Congenital Diaphragmatic Hernia in June of 2011. As I type, he is home. Taking a nap in his own crib, in his own house, thanks to all the remarkable nurses and doctors at Cincinnati Children's Hospital Medical Center.

This site will be used to educate, inform, and update the happenings at the Roettgers' House. It will be about our struggles and triumphs with CDH, a little advice and tips on parenting (as we make them up), and an overall update of Jack and his adventure in this world.

We hope that this site will help many families see into the house and lives of one great success story. This is in no way a site giving medical advice. We don't know everything about parenting or CDH, but we know Jack.

Matt and Kaytee used the blog as a form of therapy, a way of getting some of the pent-up feelings out of them. Answering the same questions over and over was emotionally draining, so a blog would give them a single voice to respond to inquiries without having to relive the unpleasant memories repeatedly. Kaytee also reached out to some online support groups for parents with chronically ill children for additional counsel and encouragement.

A few days after the blog's inception, Jack had a substantial acid reflux scare. He was fussy during the day and awake throughout the night. Jack refused to eat, relying solely on his feeds from a gastric feeding tube.

Kaytee felt frustrated and defeated. She tried to stop her "Why us?" thinking, to not get angry at Jack or at God. She says faith and her husband got her through: "Matt was patient and confident. He wasn't frustrated like me; at least he didn't show it." She was grateful to have his support, especially for the sleepless nights.

Roe hid his worry from Kaytee, but he felt lonely on the drive home from the hospital each night, often after midnight: "I was there for Kaytee, but during those nights there was no one there for me. I was all alone. It was very difficult."

Sensing this, his mom sat him down. Although Roe had to focus on his son, she was still Matt's mother. He got the message that his mom was behind him no matter what.

A few days after the acid reflux episode, Jack began gaining weight and his doctors were pleased with the results of an MRI. They did insist Jack wear a soft helmet for "flat-head syndrome," which resulted from him being bedridden so long. For the next three months, he had to wear his helmet— Cincinnati Reds-themed, naturally—23 hours a day.

Jack still needed oxygen and continuous feeding 24 hours a day through a gastric tube, but his development was going well and he even began eating some applesauce. Jack often cracked himself up by making farting noises with his tongue, resulting in belly laughs that brought smiles to his parents' faces. (I know this made Roe proud…like father, like son.)

Jack's progress continued and he was taken off his nasal cannula. He started eating pureed fruit and often slept through the night, much to Matt and Kaytee's glee. Their "delightful" boy moved his feet a mile a minute and was interactive with them. The new parents were tickled with how things were going, all things considered, and Jack's blonde hair, blue eyes, and slightly mischievous smile melted most hearts even if they were unaware of all he'd already been through in his short life.

One issue giving them fits, though, was Jack's ileostomy bag. This pouch was attached to the end of his small intestine, which protruded a bit from his stomach, to collect intestinal waste. The bag fell off repeatedly, at one point five times in 36 hours. [Kaytee asked me to mention the ostomy bag was a complication of Jack's surgery and not of CDH. She doesn't want CDH parents to think they will have to deal with an ostomy bag.]

In the summer of 2012, doctors finally agreed that Jack's small intestine could be reconnected and the bag could be removed. On June 7, Jack had "takedown surgery," his 12th operation. Jack's intestine was healthy enough for the desired repairs, and the procedure was a success. On their blog, Matt and Kaytee shared a picture of Jack post-op—he was pumping his fist in the air as if to declare: "I did it! No more ostomy bag!"

Jack spent a few days recovering in the hospital, much more at ease now without the pouch. Kaytee beams as she says, "He has been pooping from the butt ever since…YES!" For Jack's parents, after dealing with his inner organs being on the outside, changing diapers satisfied them. Jack was also showing four teeth. (I know Roe was counting the days until he could devour extra-hot chicken wings with his son.)

Matt posted a tribute to his wife on their blog:

> I am going to take this time to praise my wonderful wife…Watching her fight for Jack and this family is extremely inspirational. Between her working at her job and constantly in contact with anyone or any organization involved in Jack's well-being, she is a marvel to see in action. I am sure everyone at Children's Hospital can attest to that.
>
> I am starting to get this parenting thing down, but Jack and I would be lost puppies without Kaytee. She is truly the glue that keeps our happy little family together. So there is a reason why Jack is such a "Bad Ass." It is because his mom is the "Queen of Bad Asses." I love you, Kaytee, very much. Thanks for being such a wonderful wife and mother to our son.

On August 4, 2012, "Team Jack" hosted its first CDH Awareness Blood Drive at Holy Trinity Church in Norwood, Ohio. The Roettgerses wanted to raise awareness of CDH, while at the same time donating blood to replace the 25 pints Jack had used. They collected 28.

On August 10, Jack went to the cardiac catheter lab at Cincinnati Children's Hospital. A catheter was threaded through his thigh up into his heart. Doctors wanted to check the pressures in his heart and surrounding vessels. This was the 15th time Jack had been under anesthesia in nine months. The results were better than anticipated for a CDH baby, relieving Jack's doctors and parents that there was no cause for concern.

Jack had another appointment on August 23 to check his progress. He had gained weight steadily since the takedown surgery, and his height and weight were both in the 50th percentile, up from the 13th to 26th percentile not too long ago. Kaytee says Jack "is average to above average for CDH babies who spent time on ECMO," which was wonderful; the doctor acknowledged he would have been content with the 10th percentile.

Assured Jack was healthy enough for air travel, the family of three flew to Siesta Key, Florida, at the beginning of September with Kaytee's parents. They passed out goodie bags for fellow passengers that read: "He could be good; he could be bad. We are sorry if he makes you mad." (How cute and thoughtful is that?!)

Other than one outburst on the flight down, Jack was a trooper. The group had a great time and Jack loved the beach. He even enjoyed eating sand, which Kaytee later found out causes monumental diaper rash.

Back home again, "Team Jack" participated in the 2012 Cincinnati Walks for Kids on October 20 to raise money for kids at Cincinnati Children's Hospital. Matt and Kaytee designated their donations for the CDH Research Team, the group that helped save Jack's life. They raised more than $1,750.

At Halloween, Jack was dressed up like a Cincinnati Bengals tiger. Cold and rainy weather kept him from trick-or-treating, but he enjoyed seeing the ghosts and goblins stopping at his house for candy.

Matt and Kaytee celebrated Jack's first birthday on November 7, 2012. At Thanksgiving, Kaytee gushed: "I am most thankful for my family. If I were to lose everything but still have my family, I would still have everything."

By December, the family had settled into a nice routine and was enjoying a "mundane" life. They had no appointments or major scares. That changed on January 3, 2013, when Jack had a serious episode of croup.

Matt was playing basketball with friends when Kaytee woke up to hear the eerie sound of wheezing, which she recognized as croup from previous experience. However, this time Jack went silent. Terrified, Kaytee called 911 frantically and rushed Jack outside into the cold in an effort to kick start his breathing. She prayed for help, "even if it meant taking care of him in heaven."

Jack wasn't responding. Kaytee panicked, crying hysterically and pleading with him to breathe. Luckily, when she flipped the outdoor light switch on so the ambulance could spot them, the flash of light startled Jack. He gasped for air and howled. Kaytee was never more relieved to hear her son cry. He was taken to Cincinnati Children's Hospital and given an oral steroid and an epinephrine treatment, which cleared him up almost instantly.

Jack's one-year anniversary of being home was March 21, 2013. His original 11 medications had decreased to two. He was ostomy bag-free and no longer needed oxygen. Kaytee said having him around the house seemed so natural. She reflected on the past year: "I have thoroughly enjoyed this past year learning who you are and am looking forward to spending the rest of my life seeing who you become."

By mid-April, Jack was crawling, pulling himself up on furniture, and climbing the stairs. His motivation to get up the steps was a new playroom on the second floor. To combat Jack's explorations, Matt and Kaytee decided to invest in some baby gates.

On July 10, 2013, a representative from the NICU at Children's Hospital notified Roe and Kaytee they had put a plaque on their wall to honor Jack. Their brave boy would be one of the featured "success stories." At the Second Annual CDH Awareness Blood Drive at Holy Trinity Church, "Team Jack" donated 17 units of blood on August 3, 2013.

Jack continued to increase his intake of solid foods. He enjoyed chocolate milk, French fries dipped in ranch dressing, strawberries, ice cream, cheese, hot dogs, and chicken nuggets.

In mid-September, a cardiology appointment confirmed Jack's height and weight had improved vastly. He was now up to 24 pounds, 6 ounces. His heart was functioning normally and there was no sign of pulmonary hypertension—reassuring, because that's the main reason CDH babies fail during this phase.

Jack had surgery to rebuild his hip on November 26. As always, Jack was a warrior and the surgery corrected his left hip socket and femur successfully. Jack went home the day after Thanksgiving in a full-body cast, stylish orange and black in honor of the Cincinnati Bengals. He was "casted from armpit to toes" for three months to keep his hips and legs from moving after the surgery.

As usual, Jack was tough and patient, the latter an attribute his mother swears he didn't get from her. He enjoyed Christmas, especially lying under the tree and looking up at the lights. (Hey, there's not a lot a little dude can do in a full-body cast!) Jack also amused his parents with an obsession with Mickey Mouse and The Three Musketeers.

As expected, Jack was thrilled to get out of his cast. X-rays showed his hip was still in the socket and was doing well. Jack was transitioned into a brace to protect his hip. For three months, he was in the brace 23 hours a day. Despite the brace, Jack learned quickly how to army crawl to get around. His dad said, beaming, "Jack will be all put together by summertime…for good."

The plan was for Jack to get a stent inserted in his heart to straighten out his aorta in 2016. (Roe says this procedure sounds worse than it actually is.) However, Jack has been growing well and without complications, so the doctors are putting it off and will reassess in April 2017. The stent should be the last major surgery for Jack.

Matt and Kaytee knew the first three to four years would be challenging, but they also knew Jack's life should get much easier after that period. A cardiologist will continue to monitor Jack for several years, his goal being "to make sure his heart is good for 95 years." Jack is estimated to have half lung capacity currently, but the hope is his lungs will continue to build up and be fully developed by the time he is 9 years old.

Kaytee thinks back to the day Jack was taken off ECMO:

"Jack is on his way to a healthy and 'normal' life (what is normal, really?). Though his attitude and feistiness probably saved his life that day, he still defies the slightest assistance after surgeries. He still holds his breath and desaturates. But who am I to coach him on his use of stubborn behavior?"

As for Jack's parents, Kaytee learned her husband is a steady, level-headed support, "a lot calmer than me under pressure." Matt saw a vulnerable side of Kaytee he hadn't seen before, which made him love her even more. The ordeal brought them closer, made them see how well they work together.

Matt explains:

"A lot of couples talk a good game, but if anything is going to test a marriage, it's something like this. Communication is the key, especially with life-and-death decisions. It is cliché, but you truly learn not to take anything for granted in life.

It was tough. But it truly was a gift, a miracle, because we didn't know if we'd get a chance to be Jack's parents."

Kaytee continues: "All babies are miracles; some just have to work at it harder than others. Jack can be a handful all day and then do one thing to make it all worth it."

Matt: "We came out of this very strong. We also got to see who our real friends are."

Kaytee: "Yeah, we are lucky to have a great supporting cast. And we couldn't have asked for better doctors."

They count their blessings that they live in Cincinnati, home to one of the top hospitals for children in the world. In fact, one of the families Roe and Kaytee saw at the hospital had come all the way from Dubai.

Matt added: "Science definitely helped, but I really think that it also helped so much that his parents and family were around every day. Some of the other kids in there had no one visiting."

Matt and Kaytee felt from the beginning that if they could just get Jack out of the NICU, then he could live a long, full, and productive life. They knew they faced a struggle. But, Kaytee pronounced, "If there's a chance, we have to give it to him."

Jack is thriving now. He likes to utter the phrase from the TV commercials, "Hot pockets!" Roe says his son is more susceptible to illness and doctors won't allow him to play contact sports when he gets older, but that's OK. "I will be that parent getting emotional at every milestone," he admits.

"When he gets his first base hit, I will be crying…[big swallow]…because at one point I didn't know if I'd ever get to see him play baseball."

It wasn't long ago that Jack was hooked to ECMO, that he had multiple surgeries involving his diaphragm, bowels, heart, and lungs. But each time the doctors were done with him, Matt says Jack would just laugh. "He is the happiest little boy…and a bad ass."

On June 10, 2015, Jack Roettgers returned to Cincinnati Children's Hospital for surgery to take out the screws in his left hip and to repair an inguinal hernia. "He did so well, Jack was released from the hospital later that day," Kaytee recalls. "All three of us were so happy that we didn't have to spend another night in the hospital." Since the removal of the screws, Jack has been quite active. He especially enjoys golf and baseball.

Jack began preschool on December 2, 2014. "Though we were originally trying to get Jack enrolled in a medically sensitive preschool program, he was too healthy and developmentally caught up to be accepted," Kaytee says. "Rather, he was accepted into a mixed class with both typical kids and kids with developmental delays." Jack loves preschool.

Doctors informed Kaytee she could try to have one more child. The first pregnancy was too rough on her for any more. My friends, as usual, took the news in stride. "If it is meant to be, great; if not, we already have this little guy," Matt said at the time.

Thankfully, the Roettgers family found out in the spring of 2015 that Jack was going to be a big brother. Max Roettgers was born on November 29, 2015. The proud parents report that both the boys are doing well. "They are in daycare so they are constantly wiping their noses," Kaytee says, "but nothing too serious."

Jack is finishing his first year of tee ball—he had a blast—and is going to play soccer next. Max is growing fast and is getting his third tooth. Kaytee says he's a very happy baby and loves his big brother.

For Jack's second birthday, Kaytee wrote this blog post:

> Happy Birthday, Jack. You are growing into a wonderful and smart little boy. You have come a LONG way in the past two years, and I am looking forward to many, many more years of watching you heal, grow, and learn.
>
> I love you with all my heart and soul.

Yes, their story is about a brave boy, but it is also about love and a pretty amazing family.

....

You can find more information, including YouTube videos, on Matt and Kaytee's blog, weknowjackdotme.wordpress. com. If you would like to make a donation in honor of Jack Roettgers, please do so at Ronald McDonald House Charities of Greater Cincinnati (www.rmhcincinnati.org) or Cincinnati Children's Hospital Medical Center (www. cincinnatichildrens.org).

J

Helen and Joseph McMahon welcomed "J" into the world on November 30, 1947, at Jewish Hospital in Cincinnati, Ohio. Joe was a pipe fitter and Helen a secretary, in a time before a mother working was common. Helen's mother lived with them as well, so J and her younger brother had a built-in babysitter. Because Helen worked, J's grandmother took care of the cooking, making simple, basic meals.

They didn't own a car back then, so the McMahon family often would take the bus to the Cincinnati Zoo, Eden Park, or Coney Island. They moved a lot during J's childhood often renting apartments and two-family houses. One in particular stands out in J's mind because the living room also doubled as her parents' bedroom—they slept on a pullout couch while J, her brother, and her grandmother shared the bedroom. In grade school, J enjoyed climbing trees, playing four-square and other games with the neighborhood kids, and packing a lunch to take along to the pool in Oakley. She loved reading, especially Nancy Drew and the Boxcar Children books, and hoped to be a teacher when she grew up.

One day, out of nowhere, everything changed.

While Helen was at work, she began to have severe stomach pain, and an ambulance was summoned. Unbeknownst to Helen's mother and children, Helen was pregnant. She'd had a tubal pregnancy, long before sonograms could detect them easily. J's mother died on the way to the hospital.

Helen was only 40 years old.

J was not yet 9, her brother 3.

J came home from school and was told the news, and a neighbor rocked her for a long time on the front porch. J and her family were stunned.

When J returned to school, no one mentioned her mother's death, not even J's teachers. They just stared at her. J recalls, "I wish someone would have acknowledged the loss, and then we could have moved on." The experience left J embarrassed, sad, and wishing she could shrink into the floor. She felt disillusioned, that life was no longer good and fair.

J had adored her mother, who was pretty, slightly overweight, and always nicely dressed. After Helen's untimely death, her family rarely did anything together. J's father took her roller skating on Saturday nights for a few years, but their lone bonding time ended when the rink shut down. (J doesn't recollect her father taking her brother anywhere.) Her father barely left the house except to go to work.

J's father and grandmother never got along, but they couldn't stand each other after Helen's death. J's grandmother was impatient and negative. She was "flat-out mean" to J's father, which led to constant tension in the house. Her father tried to ignore his mother-in-law, so they usually didn't even speak to one another. Her grandmother was stoutly anti-Catholic, but her father had been a non-practicing Catholic for years. However, they needed each other to get by—J's grandmother needed a place to live and her dad needed someone to help with the kids.

The death of J's mother "changed everything, all for the worse. It made me grow up faster than I should have," J says. J basically became her brother's surrogate mother, though she was only five and a half years his senior. She recalls being sent downtown with her brother to buy him school clothes when she was just 13. J still regrets not being nicer to him but realizes she was simply too young to be a mother-figure.

By high school, J had even more responsibility around the house. Her father and grandmother were both too old and tired, so J did most of the grocery shopping, cleaning, ironing, and laundry. She used her $5 allowance to pay the bus fare to school and to buy milk at lunch. She used the rest of her money to take baton lessons.

Looking back, J says her family was fairly poor, but she didn't realize it at the time. As a teenager, she was embarrassed by her "shoddy" home, often sacrificing her allowance to purchase small things for the house. She learned to be thrifty and can't stand pretense to this day.

J's father basically just went to work and came home. He went to the grocery store about once a week and dropped off J and her brother at a Protestant church on Sundays. He spent the hour at a bar around the corner from the church and then picked up his children.

J's dad eventually started leaving the house dressed up on Saturday nights without explanation. Actually, he never talked to the family about much of anything. J found out years later her dad tried dating for several months, but in the end, "he just couldn't do it." J still doesn't know if dating hadn't worked out for her father due to his familial obligations or because he had lost the one true love of his life.

J's brother's story is even more tragic. By his teens, he got a little wild, often sneaking off in the family car to joyride at night. He wrecked a few vehicles, but "my grandma spoiled him rotten," J says. Her brother graduated high school and joined the Air Force. He got married and was sent to Japan, where he had two children.

By the time he was sent back home, J's brother was drinking heavily, and a divorce soon followed. He moved somewhere out west and J never heard from him again. Even now, so many years later, J would like to know what happened to him, but she has been unable to track him down. She wonders if her brother is dead or alive.

J said carrying on after her mother died was the hardest thing she's ever had to do. "Life was very different after that." She lost out on having a "normal" family, one that went places together and had company come over to visit. Instead, J envied friends and classmates who had both of their parents and who did things collectively as a family.

Every summer, J would get to stay with her mother's family in Dayton, Ohio, for one week. She loved being around a traditional family. One of her favorite memories is getting to tag along when two families rented a beach house—eight people riding up to Cape Cod, Massachusetts, in a station wagon, the first time J had ever been out of the Cincinnati and Dayton area.

At Lyon Junior High and Withrow High School, J had good friends and was active as a baton-twirling majorette and as part of the Dance Club. She was also a member of "Dux Femina," an honorary society of the top 12 girls in her class based on grades, citizenship, and activities. But her favorite affiliation was the "Out for Fun Club," a group of female friends that became the closest thing to a family for J. She often served as the club's president.

Whereas her father and brother never seemed to recover, J pulled through. She credits her strict church upbringing and being active in school for keeping her on the correct path. J also feels fortunate to have had nice, clean-cut friends to help her through tough times.

During junior high and high school, J spent a lot of time at her best friend, Johanna's, house. J met Johanna's brother Patrick in the seventh grade. Though she thought "Pat" was cute and athletic, he ignored J until she was in high school. But he ended up outgrowing his indifference and they began dating.

J and Pat married on June 6, 1968. They got a small, one-bedroom apartment in a 16-unit building and had a baby girl. When their daughter was 1, they moved to a more kid-friendly, two-bedroom apartment; the neighbors above and below them in their first apartment would pound on the floor or ceiling whenever the baby cried.

J and Pat had another girl, then a boy, and finally a second boy. J and Pat raised their four kids on Pat's teacher salary. During the summer, Pat made extra money as an assistant manager at a swim club and coached many of the kids' teams in sports. J was a stay-at-home mom, Girl Scout leader, and PTA president. When the kids were grown, she went back to school to get her associate's degree in accounting, earning straight A's. For 20 years, she worked as an accountant and bookkeeper before retiring at the beginning of 2013.

To keep busy post-retirement—J *always* feels she has to be doing something, which she attributes to having so much responsibility early on in her life—she volunteers at Christ Hospital, babysits grandchildren, and attends a nondenominational church. J also stays active at a fitness club and enjoys finding bargains at garage sales. She is so skilled with coupons and finding deals that I suspect grocery stores owe her money by the time she's done shopping.

From her burdensome childhood, J learned self-reliance, but she also had to grow up too fast. As an adult, a friend told her she has "an overdeveloped sense of responsibility." J says the happiest time in her life was when her kids were young, because she felt the most useful, the most important to someone.

She has been useful and important to many people. I should know—J actually goes by "Jolinda," but I've always called her "Mom."

Often I find the smaller the person, the bigger the heart. Standing 5 feet, 4 inches and with short, black hair, my mom is almost a saint. Nearly everything she does is for someone else.

My three siblings and I never knew much about my mom's painful childhood, because she didn't talk about her youth. She probably thought she would be burdening us. Though she realizes being put into that role so young wasn't fair to her or her brother, my mom laments not doing a better job with him. I remind my mom she was not even a teenager at the time.

My mom yearned to be a stay-at-home mother; she always hated that her mother worked during her childhood. She also vowed long ago to be unlike her grandmother. My mom wants to be remembered primarily as a good mother; she has achieved this many times over.

For my 25th birthday, my mom gave me the most special present I've ever received. She had compiled a photo album of my life from the day I was born until my quarter-century mark—my first day of kindergarten, family trips, sporting events, high school prom, college graduation, etc.

She also included a card from her and my dad telling me they were proud of me and loved me. When it sank in just how much time, devotion, and sacrifice she took making this thoughtful, selfless gift, tears came to my eyes. What a wonderful memento I can share with my own family someday.

Who works on a gift for someone for that long? A mother. No greater love exists in the world than a mother's love.

When asked what would be the best gift she could receive, she replied in typical fashion:

"It wouldn't be a tangible thing. It would be the assurance that all my children and their spouses would stay healthy and happy and all our grandkids would grow up to be healthy, happy people. I just want all of them to have good lives. Everyone has issues and difficulties, but I hope they can all get past those things and thrive."

Some of the important lessons Jolinda has learned are that we don't always get what we want; some things just can't be explained (her mother's untimely death, for example); there's no friend like an old friend; friends come and go, but your family is always family; and the people in your life are far more important than material things. My mom says good health, faith in God (or some spiritual fulfillment), a feeling of purpose, and people whom you love and who love you are life's greatest gifts.

Her advice:

"Do the best with what you've got. We don't all get to start life in ideal conditions. And there will always be someone smarter, richer, better-looking, and more talented than we are. By the same token, there will always be many people a whole lot less fortunate than we are.

"So, do your best, behave, and try to help others along the way. You have to laugh at yourself. If you can't laugh at yourself, you are trying to be perfect and that's not possible."

For the past few years, my mom and dad have enjoyed taking bus tours. They spend a lot of time watching their eight grandkids, which makes them both happy. They are superb grandparents and attend many of the kids' school functions and sporting events.

My mom's previous employer called her out of retirement to help for a while, but she has since re-retired. She volunteers one day a week at Christ Hospital and once a month at Matthew 25: Ministries, a humanitarian aid organization based in Cincinnati. My mom and dad play bridge at a senior citizen center every Tuesday.

Not long ago, I hugged my mom and told her I was sorry to hear about what she had gone through. She cried for maybe two seconds before making herself stop. My heart broke when I realized her mother's death still hurts more than 55 years later.

When I first asked my mom to be a part of this book, she was willing but didn't think her story was worth telling because she hadn't gone on to do great things with her life. I countered that she had raised four good kids. My oldest sister is a mother of four and a former pharmacist who now cares for the elderly; my other sister is a mother of two and a special needs teacher; and my brother is a father of two who earned a Green Beret with the U.S. Army Special Forces and currently works as a firefighter and paramedic when he is not serving with the National Guard. Furthermore, Mom's children have produced eight extraordinary grandchildren.

I would say my mom has done plenty.

....

If you would like to make a donation in honor of Jolinda Maginn, please do so at Matthew 25: Ministries (www. m25m.org).

Joy

Over and over again, Joy Ward felt she had to do something differently. Joy had worked for her family's businesses since she was 13 years old. The free spirit with long, strawberry-blonde hair, sparkling blue eyes, and a smile that spreads to everyone in the room wasn't sure what she wanted to do, but she knew it wasn't catering for the rest of her life. Yet Joy didn't feel confident in any other area.

After graduating from Oak Hills High School in 1999, Joy went to Bowling Green State University in northern Ohio but got homesick and returned to Cincinnati. She enrolled in Antonelli College and earned an associate's degree in photography. From there, Joy got a bachelor of fine arts degree at the College of Mount Saint Joseph, where she also played soccer.

Throughout high school and college, Joy spent weekends and most of the holidays working alongside her parents and three older siblings. "Catering is what I know best," she says. "It's comfortable and I'm good at it."

Joy's parents, Nancy and Tom Ward, first met while working in food and beverage at a hotel. After marriage and two children, Holly and Adam, the Wards decided to open a restaurant. The couple had no experience running a busi-ness whatsoever—and Nancy was pregnant—but they went ahead anyway. While cooking at the restaurant on opening day, Nancy went into labor with Joy's sister Jill.

The restaurant led to the catering business, which led to running a banquet hall, The Meadows. When the Wards sold the hall, Joy's dad took on the contract of running the food service at the Sharonville Convention Center as Village Pantry Catering. At the same time, Joy's mom ran RSVP Event Center a banquet facility, and handled the Village Pantry's off-site catering. Joy and her three siblings all worked together in some capacity, and the Wards managed to get along quite well while being around each other almost constantly.

Joy's family has always had a good work ethic, but they also know how to relax and enjoy life away from the job. Much of their focus has been on making sure people have an enjoyable time, so for the Wards to have fun when they're off the clock is not too much of a stretch. "When it's time to have a party of our own," Joy says, grinning, "we go all out." (I can attest to this, as Jill and Joy had some of the best high school parties.)

Joy genuinely enjoyed her job, especially her fellow staff. "Catering is hard work," she admits, "but working with remarkable coworkers makes it so much better." Yet Joy ached for a change.

With this stirring in her mind, Joy also was looking for a

way to deepen her yoga practice, which her mom had introduced her to about 12 years earlier. Joy found yoga boring at first but soon realized there was far more to the discipline than she originally had thought. Jill, a yoga instructor, also inspired and encouraged Joy's love of yoga.

Joy learned that yoga and healthy eating are an excellent combination for enhancing mental clarity and happiness—in other words, feeling well in mind, body, and soul. Yoga teacher training interested her, so she looked for a program in the Cincinnati area that might be a good fit. But the local schools offered training only one weekend a month for an entire year, and Joy worked on the weekends.

Joy wanted to be tested in her yoga practice and in her life in general. The family businesses were all she had ever known, but Joy sensed there was much more to experience outside of her comfort zone. She didn't want to know what she was getting herself into…and she wanted to be OK with the uncertainty. If she didn't quit her job then, Joy reasoned, she never would.

In addition to a strong work ethic, Tom and Nancy Ward also instilled their passion for travelling in their children. "They brought us kids along on their travels as often as they could take off work," Joy recalls. "They were a big influence for my love for travel and have also encouraged us to see the beauty of the world as much as we could."

During the summer of 2013, Joy met her sister Holly in Lake Tahoe, California, at the Wanderlust Festival, a celebration of music and yoga. Joy then spent 10 days, mostly by herself, driving through California to Washington and then back down the coast. She camped and visited friends along the way and loved the adventure, which provided even more ammunition for her restlessness.

Joy yearned to meet new people, to have new escapades. This perfect storm of wanting more out of life, her need to break from her longtime job, and her desire for personal growth through yoga was finally too much to ignore. Though giving her three months' notice at work—Joy wanted to give them plenty of time to find a replacement—was emotional for her, Joy took a leap of faith.

"I decided to start 2014 with yoga teacher training in Nicaragua," says Joy. Something about Nica Yoga in southwest Nicaragua appealed to her, because the other retreats she found online looked too commercial, too perfect. Joy had no idea what she would do once the three-week teacher training was over, but she trusted things would come together.

Joy and I come from the conservative Midwestern United States, a region where people work hard and, for better or worse, often don't stray too far from home. Cincinnatians, in particular, have a reputation for never leaving our hometown. This tendency is probably common for many areas of the country, actually. For example, when I went on a pay-it-forward road trip around the southeast for a few weeks, over and over people said they'd always wanted to move elsewhere, to see the world. But, for whatever reason, they never had.

Joy, on the other hand, listened to her heart and left her comfort zone. She felt there was more to life than what she was experiencing, and she went looking. Her courage is admirable. I realize Joy didn't face major adversity the way others in this book did, but I included her because I respect her for taking a leap of faith and for being true to herself. She felt a major change was necessary and had the guts to follow through.

Joy's parents have a villa in Nicaragua, which was one option, but otherwise her itinerary was up to chance. This would terrify many people, but Joy shook off the anxiety. "I had little fears, but I told myself that they weren't real," she says. "Things started falling into place and I kept getting signs and reassurance from things that happened, things that I read." For example, Joy noticed she got bigger tips than usual during her last month of work. "Everything kept working itself out."

Before her trek, family, friends, and coworkers took Joy out to a casino for a night of fun. On New Year's Day 2014, the Ward family had dinner together. Joy's sister Holly posted a Facebook comment—"We will miss you, Joy!!! I admire you so much for following your dreams. Can't wait to hear all about it! Lots of love and prayers for you!"—along with a quote from Dr. Martin Luther King, Jr.: "Faith is taking the first step, even when you don't see the whole staircase."

Joy flew to Nicaragua's capital city, Managua, on January 3. She was thrilled to meet new people, spend time in nature, learn, and grow. Joy compared the feeling to leaving for summer camp as a kid, which she had loved. Joy realized there was no turning back when she tried to check into her hotel upon landing. "I was just a dumb American," she laughs. "I don't even speak Spanish."

Managua is two hours from San Juan del Sur, where her yoga teacher training would begin in two days. Joy and one of the other students, Jacq (pronounced "Jack"), stayed at the same hotel prior to training, so they shared a taxi to Nica Yoga on January 5. When they arrived, Joy and Jacq were pleased to discover they had been paired as roommates. Though they had just met, Joy said it was as if they'd known each other for years.

Nica Yoga is a picturesque retreat nestled in the hills about three miles from San Juan del Sur, a coastal town and popular tourist vacation spot on the Pacific Ocean. Surrounded by nature, the grounds include a spacious, open-air yoga studio ("Shala"), a pool, and cozy housing. In addition to Joy, seven other women from all over the United States and Canada showed up for the course. The two instructors came in from Arizona and North Carolina and, though total opposites, were remarkable. Joy felt she could not have picked better people. In truth, Joy loved all Nica Yoga had to offer: "Everything is wonderful…instructors, students, FOOD, sun, animals, the breeze…magnífico!!!"

Training was held every day except Sunday. The students rose early, expected to be on time for the first session at 6:30 a.m. After two hours of yoga, the group ate breakfast, observing "noble silence" each morning until 10:30 a.m. Joy quickly got used to the mandated quiet, which enabled her other senses to be heightened. She listened to the birds and monkeys playing in the trees nearby. After a lot of yoga instruction, meditation, and an evening lecture, the day ended at 9 p.m. and the students had the rest of the night to read, watch a movie, or study their yoga manuals.

On January 8, Joy taunted family and friends back in Cincinnati, Ohio—enduring one of the coldest, snowiest winters on record—with pictures of her sunny paradise: "Learning so much in this beautiful Shala with beautiful people. Surrounded by nature the entire day…LOVING it!!"

One of the highlights of Joy's time at Nica occurred midway through the training when a group of about 14 kids from a local orphanage visited for the day. A boy named Oscar scarcely left Joy's side throughout the entire day. The two groups spent time on the beach, ate ice cream, did yoga, and swam in Nica's pool before the youngsters headed home after a fun, full day. Though Joy and her fellow trainees could barely communicate with the orphans verbally, their time together was a special occurrence.

A post from January 24 exemplifies Joy's mindset at Nica:

Enjoying where I am on the way to where I am going. Feeling very grateful today! I haven't worked in 24 days…that is the longest I have gone since I was 13 years old. That makes me happy and I still have many more days ahead to work on myself rather than go to work. Smiling big with lots of gratitude!!!

Though they came to Nica Yoga from different places and had unique stories, Joy and the other women got along well. Personal emotions often came up, but everyone let their guards down and opened up. "We were digging deep," Joy remembers, "and in many ways I feel like we knew more about each other than some of my friends back home."

Joy's classmate Cynthia summed up the training eloquently:

> We are nearing the end of our time here at Nica Yoga. Today is our last day, and our ceremony will be held tonight. Our intimate group of only eight ladies has proved to be an experience like no other. We have watched, listened, learned, laughed, and surrendered our innermost challenges and fears with each other. We have struggled physically and emotionally, and we have found truth, amongst laughter and tears, often tears of utmost joy…this experience will always be cherished in our hearts.

The women celebrated their accomplishment together at a ceremony on January 29. The yoginis received a certificate enabling them to register with Yoga Alliance, verifying they were qualified to spread their love of yoga to others. The students were now teachers.

Joy beamed:

> Yoga Teacher Training Complete. What an amazing experience! I went in with no expectations, except for one BIG one…that it will change my life… and that has proven to be true. What an incredible program, with amazing women in the beautiful jungle…I could not have asked for anything more. I'm not sure how I got here, but I did, and it was exactly where I was supposed to be. Excited to travel on through Nicaragua for another month!! Thanks and love to all who have supported me.

With training behind her, Joy had a few weeks in Nicaragua to do whatever she wanted. She spent the first night in Granada, Nicaragua, with some of her classmates from the retreat. Joy and Cynthia then headed to Joy's parents' villa in an area called Laguna de Apoyo, part of the Apoyo Lagoon Natural Reserve, an hour outside of Managua. Nancy and Tom Ward joined them two days later, and the foursome went to Granada to shop and sight-see and then spent time on the lake.

Lindsey, another friend from training, arrived on February 3. The next day, the group went for a boat ride on Lake Nicaragua where they saw "beautiful homes, not-so-beautiful homes, birds, cute monkeys, and lush greenery." Joy, her parents, and friends spent the following day relaxing at the lake before taking a Thai cooking class.

Though sad to see her mom and dad go on February 6, venturing on with Lindsey excited Joy. This "amazing and interesting" friend, who had worked and saved up enough money to travel for three years straight, inspired her. On February 9, Lindsey led Joy on the latter's first real back-packing quest.

Joy had agreed to go before she knew what she was getting herself into. She was somewhat worried when Lindsey asked, "Are you ready for this?" Lindsey knew just enough Spanish to make some sense at the bus stops, which Joy describes as madness. Drivers grabbed at their bags, trying to persuade the Americans to get into their cabs. One offered to take them to the beach that moment for $10, which sounded good to Joy since the next bus wasn't coming for a few hours. But Lindsey was about the adventure—and doing so on the cheap—so they waited at the bus stop and filled the time reading and journaling.

Their bus finally arrived but was so packed with people that the driver wouldn't allow them to get on. Though he tried to leave without Lindsey and Joy, they caught up to the bus and squeezed into what little space remained. They wouldn't be denied—not only had they waited three long hours, Joy and Lindsey already had stowed their bags on top of the bus! Loud music blared from the speakers, the sweaty passengers so cramped hardly anyone could move.

Somehow the pair reached exquisite Jiquilillo Beach. To Joy's delight, they found a vegetarian beach hostel run by "a total stoner hippie lady" from San Francisco and bunked in a room with six others. Their host warned them to return before dark, as the beach was unsafe at night. In fact, some girls from the hostel got robbed by a man with a hammer on the second night of Joy and Lindsey's stay.

An easier day of travel on February 11 brought them to their next stop, the stunning city of León, Nicaragua. Joy put a picture of the "adorable" hostel on Facebook and proclaimed: "Our home for 3 nights. $7 a night, $1 beers on honor system, free coffee, free breakfast. I love Central America!!" They enjoyed a volcano tour about an hour from León, which tested their nerve when they realized they had to sled down the volcano side on wooden boards.

Joy found León gorgeous and was delighted to have met some great people. Joy continually felt everyone she encountered on her trip was fascinating, while she was always the one who'd done the least in her life: *I have nothing to share, just catering and Cincinnati. Think about all of the cool places they've been…and they all speak three languages.* Indeed, one asserted, "Americans don't travel; they stay at home watching *Family Guy*."

But Joy was pleased that her travelling companion was adventurous. When given the choice, Lindsey would opt for the more daring alternative. Instead of taking a boring taxi to their next location, for example, the pair took two chicken buses, two cabs, an airplane, and a boat to get to Little Corn Island, where they reunited with Jacq, Joy's roommate from yoga teacher training.

Jacq had just moved to this gorgeous island and greeted her guests with beer in hand. Joy's initial fears that nine days here might be too long were immediately silenced: "Loving this life and feeling so peaceful and grateful." (Lindsey actually stayed a day longer than she had planned because she lost track of the days and missed her flight.)

Two days later, Joy flew back to her parents' place in Managua for one more week alone in Nicaragua. She did yoga every morning, went for runs, relaxed at the lake, and cooked, but Joy was going a bit stir-crazy by herself. She hadn't spoken English in days and was ready to get back to the United States just to talk to someone.

On her last night in Nicaragua, Joy reflected:

> I'm feeling very blessed for the amazing 8 weeks and all of the experiences I have had in this country. It also saddens me to realize how many conveniences and luxuries I take for granted every day in the US, and all of the things I expect and don't think twice about having. Things that I will not miss about being here are difficulties most of the people here face every day. I will not miss the smell of garbage burning, hand washing my clothes, worry of clean water supply, lack of access to any food I want, unpaved bumpy roads, dirty feet…However, I will miss the huge welcoming smiles, warm hearts, and friendliness of the people. I will miss the exotic flowers, loud monkeys, colorful birds, volcanoes,

> warmth, water, color…I hope that the broadening
> of compassion and awareness I feel NOW will stay
> with me, and I will not slip back into the lack of
> gratitude and appreciation for all that I have.

Joy had planned originally to return to Cincinnati after Nicaragua, but she changed her mind when her sister Jill's friend Rob invited her to stay with him in Los Angeles. Rob had seen Joy's Facebook updates about her travels and suggested she extend her trip for a while. Joy wasn't ready to go home just yet, so she accepted his generous offer.

Rob wanted to make use of a tear-drop camper he had acquired recently, so he and Joy drove to Joshua Tree National Park on March 3. They dropped the camper at a campsite and went in search of hiking trails. As darkness fell, they picked a path on a whim and were treated with a stunning sunset. Joy sighs, "It was perfect how it happened, the timing, and that specific trail." Once again, things seemed to work out whenever she set out in faith.

After camping along the river on the Arizona/California border in Bull Head City, Joy and Rob decided to go to Las Vegas for a few days. Unfortunately, Joy got sick. She had no energy, exhausted from her travels.

For the lone time on her trip, Joy wanted to go home. She lay by the pool at the RV resort on the first day but spent the following day in the camper watching nine straight episodes of *Orange Is the New Black* on Rob's laptop. (To his credit, Rob didn't abandon Joy and head into Vegas on his own but stayed with her.)

By March 8, they were back in California and Joy had rallied. While biking on Venice Beach, she enjoyed seeing the street performers and "all the wild and crazy people." The next day, she explored "beautiful" Huntington Beach.

On the final night of her journey, Joy had one last post:

> 'When nothing is certain, everything is possible' pretty much sums up the past 10 weeks for me. ALL in with no expectations has worked out amazingly for me. My heart has opened, my eyes less blurred, my life is forever changed…but back to reality—I need a job!!!

Joy's trip had gone even better than she'd imagined. She'd taken a big risk stepping out of her comfort zone, but the payoff for her courage was substantial. Joy had some incredible adventures and met many interesting people.

Joy found Nicaragua to be a lovely country. She appreciated how the people live, as well as their work ethic. She marveled at the always-smiling people, admiring how they look out for each other, such as when a mother would hand her baby to a stranger on the bus while she got situated.

Home again, Joy was still unsure about her plans for the future. Along with her consistent salary, Joy had given up a few nice perks when she left her job, including health insurance. But she chose to remain calm, refusing to get caught up in worry. In any case, Joy reasoned, she wouldn't starve. She could live simply and would always have catering to go back to if necessary.

A week and a half after Joy Ward returned home from Nicaragua and California, her 63-year-old father had a massive heart attack. Tom Ward went into cardiac arrest while eating dinner with his wife and two other couples. Though two doctors were at the restaurant and performed CPR on Mr. Ward almost immediately, his outlook was not good.

His heart stopped several times throughout the next week. He spent several days in the cardiovascular intensive care unit fighting to get healthy enough to have double-bypass surgery. Mr. Ward spent 27 days at a hospital before transferring to a rehab facility. The father of four and grandfather of 11 recovered quite miraculously and is doing great. The scare brought an already close Ward family even closer.

Settled back into Cincinnati, Joy got the head coaching position for the Oak Hills High School girls' freshman soccer team, which she enjoyed greatly. She took as much pleasure in each day as possible and decided not to stress over her next move.

Joy continues a regular yoga practice but doesn't plan on teaching yoga, at least for now. Instead, Joy went through training in January 2015 to become a flight attendant. She loves that her new career allows not only more travel opportunities for her, but also for her parents, who sparked Joy's passion long ago. Naturally, Joy snuck in a two-week vacation to Nicaragua before her instruction began.

Joy relocated to Knoxville, Tennessee, for her new career with American Airlines. She enjoys being a flight attendant and has traveled around the southern and eastern United States. "I plan on using my flying benefits more to travel abroad once I gain seniority and can take more days off in a row. Japan, Italy, Ireland, and many others are on my list." Though she liked Knoxville, she was planning to move back to Cincinnati in the summer of 2016.

Wise beyond her years, Joy explains:

"I have learned to trust myself and to trust in God in many more ways than I ever could before. Learning and knowing this type of trust might have been the hardest, yet simplest thing I have learned. I may not be where I thought I would or should be in my life, but I am right where I am supposed to be, and that is awesome. I have learned that everyone is on their own unique path and it is OK that mine does not look like theirs. It is OK that I make mistakes and I don't have it all figured out. It is OK, because I am on the path of Joy—that is me and that is who I am. I can't be anyone else…I have tried…it never works. I have always felt like I was running away from something and that I was never good enough, but now I feel like I'm running toward a brighter and more abundant life…a life of freedom, faith, love, acceptance, service, joy, and happiness.

"I believe God, yoga, and love for self are essential for my path to peace. I also know I can't do this alone. My loving family, awesome friends, and supportive personal trainer have helped in more ways than they even know, and I am forever grateful. We are all here for a purpose and we all have gifts we need to share with the world. Why not search for our purpose and share our gifts? What else do we have to lose? I am searching for my purpose and praying I can share my gifts with others while trying to be a better person than I once was. This experience has opened my heart and my eyes in amazing ways. I am extremely grateful for what has been and what is to come."

....

If you would like to make a donation in honor of Joy Ward, please do so at American Heart Association (www.heart. org/HEARTORG).

Martin

Martin was about the last person I would have pegged as a recovering crack cocaine addict. I was astounded that this kind man volunteering his time to mentor me, a complete stranger, had once been hooked on such a serious drug. I wouldn't wish a drug dependency on anyone, but I was grateful to be paired with someone who was doing well after going through challenging times. This older, medium-height, African-American man with short, often shaved hair, and glasses had first-hand knowledge of being at the bottom of the ditch, so to speak. But he persevered and now gave back to other men who wanted to improve their own lives.

Martin was born in Hamilton, Ohio, in 1946. His earliest memories are fond ones of being around his grandmother, whom he adored. Martin felt security in his grandmother's love.

Sadly, Martin's grandmother passed away when Martin was 9 years old, his first experience of major loss. He believes if he would have understood what was going on, his pain might have been less profound, but Martin didn't grasp the circumstances. Being so young, he didn't comprehend that he wouldn't see his grandmother again.

Martin came from a "yes, ma'am" and "no, sir" generation when kids didn't ask questions. "All I knew was she was in a coffin and then I'm lost," Martin says. His grandmother's death caused a void in his life, initiating a sadness Martin would carry for many years.

Martin's father had turned his own life around at the age of 27. Critically ill with a freak arterial condition, his dad pleaded with God from his deathbed, "If you save me, I'll serve you." After a miraculous recovery, Martin's father made good on his promise and served as a preacher for the rest of his life, into his early 80s. "When he found the Lord as his savior," Martin recollects, "his whole life changed."

Martin's life also changed. Being the son of a preacher put a lot of pressure on him that he didn't understand at such a tender age. Quick to acknowledge he had positive guidance and the demands didn't come from his family, Martin still wanted to distance himself from the rules and do things his own way. He struggled with authority and wanted to get away.

One release was athletics. Martin's name often made the newspaper for his football and track prowess at Hamilton Garfield High School. After medaling in the 100-yard dash at one event, Martin even got to meet his idol, track legend Jesse Owens, who told him to keep up the good work. Though Martin enjoyed sports, he still fell in with the wrong crowd.

Some "party friends" introduced Martin to cigarettes,

wine, and beer when he was 18 years old. Soon thereafter, a childhood friend persuaded him to try marijuana. Martin liked these crutches immediately. "We did nothing but laugh and eat," Martin chuckles. Nevertheless, he sees in hindsight getting drunk and high was "a pacifier for my depression."

"I don't know why I chose to do those things," Martin says. "I thought it was a way of filling the void."

After he and a young woman "courted" for about a year, Martin married at the age of 21. Drafted into the Army in August 1967, Martin served as a tank driver in Germany for two years. His marriage lasted seven years, but the relationship ultimately failed. (The couple did not have children.)

"It was probably my fault," Martin repents. "She was Catholic and I was Apostolic Pentecostal. Big difference. We didn't see eye to eye on some things."

Martin had five children, some out of wedlock. He raised his kids for a few years, until the relationships with their mothers didn't work out. In 1977, he moved to Florida for a new beginning. Martin acknowledges he ran to get away from the dilemmas he'd created in his life. "I had no control over my life. I didn't want control."

Around 1980, Martin went to California and got a job at a Navy shipyard. He was exposed to pimps and drug dealers—men with loads of money who were driven around in limousines. The "bright California lights, the women, and the shiny Cadillacs" attracted Martin, and he began hustling crack cocaine.

Crack is the smokable and arguably most addictive form of cocaine. "I thought I could sell it," he sighs, "but it sold me." With crack, Martin had power over another person— the user. Conversely, the substance controlled Martin.

In 1985, Martin got gravely sick, and an artery to his heart closed. He moved home to Hamilton, wanting to get his life in order. "I was raised in the church and I knew the Lord, but I still had more soul-searching to do," Martin says.

Martin tried to quit many times, often going straight for three months at a time. Yet his "old enemy" kept returning. For three- or four-day stretches, Martin would resort to using.

At his lowest point, Martin was homeless. Rather than staying with friends and family, he slept in shelters. "I hit rock bottom. I didn't want people I knew to see me on that stuff," he explains. During the day, he would often wander around town, looking for meals in garbage cans.

His mother realized Martin had drug issues, but she didn't confront her son until she discovered he was using crack. She scolded Martin, praying he would do better while she was still alive. Letting his mother down was a crucial moment for Martin: "Lord, I really need your help. My mom's disappointed in me, so you must be, too."

When Martin was 44, he got his life together. He spent more time in church and hung around "church people." Martin discussed his demons with "a man of God that I trusted" and stopped succumbing to every impulse as he once had, asking himself, "Is this right or is this wrong?" before acting. He is thankful some people never turned their back on him, especially an aunt who showed Martin unconditional love while he was in the grip of addiction.

He wanted to change, but transformation didn't come overnight. With persistence, Martin kicked the habit in 1991 after years of struggling with crack cocaine.

He decided to enroll in cosmetology school. He'd always loved cutting family members' hair. Even at the age of 8 or 9, Martin knew he was talented working with hair. The program was intense—"Cosmetology school is rough, buddy!"—but Martin says the regimen enabled him to stay clean.

Thriving in his classes gave Martin a stronger faith and more confidence. Though he had been a "C" student in high school, Martin earned grades in the 90s. Fortunately, the years of fast living hadn't stolen his mind.

In 2003, Martin found out he had cancer. Martin quit smoking following the news. The disease spread from his kidneys to his lungs but stopped progressing after doctors removed one of Martin's kidneys. Medication has shrunk the cancer significantly, and Martin feels healthy. "I can go fly a kite now," he jokes.

About six years ago, his father saw something spiritual in Martin and made him a deacon. "He prayed, and I believe he had an insight that everything was going to be all right," Martin says. "He didn't have to worry anymore."

Back in cosmetology school, Martin made God a promise. Since he still had most of his wits despite all of the drinking and drugs, he promised to put them to good use. Martin stood by his word. He became a deacon and teaches adult Sunday school on the third weekend of every month. Martin enjoys his role because he loves being with people and is eager to learn everything he can.

Martin's passion for people brought him to the Adam Center almost four years ago. The Adam Center (adamcenters.org) is "a faith-based organization that provides men, ages 18 and older, a free, confidential place to build trust, be heard and heal. The Adam Center is intentionally designed to create an environment where non-judgmental listening, sharing, encouragement, and prayer support take place."

Martin connected with the program instantly. "I knew the Lord was in it," he declares. Sensing he had a higher purpose, Martin became a volunteer mentor. His battles with depression, hopelessness, and alcohol and drug addictions would allow him to relate to others who are struggling and need guidance.

He has been there. He understands and wants to serve. In the words of Eckhart Tolle in *The Power of Now*, Martin's past has given him "depth, humility, and compassion."

He hasn't forgotten thoughts of throwing himself off a bridge. Martin remembers taking puffs from discarded cigarette butts off the street after making sure no one was looking. Even then, Martin knew he was better than that and prayed over and over that God would rescue him.

"I went through something for a reason—to help someone else." A gentle, modest man, Martin gives the credit to God. "He brought me out and delivered me. I squandered my life, Lord knows, but I have another chance to help others."

Martin remarried six years ago to "a wonderful, itty bitty woman" named Linda. "The Lord blessed me!" he says, beaming. The two are the same age and have a lot in common. Linda has been sick with one ailment or another for much of her life, yet she, too, turned her life around.

Martin calls his wife his "help mate." They go to doctor's appointments together and look out for each other. "I never had a woman who stuck by me. She makes things better for me, feeds me right," he says.

Soon after they met, Martin invited Linda to go to church with him. She liked what she felt and heard, as well as the church family itself. Linda joined Martin's church and he proposed six months later. "I ain't gonna let a good thing get away from me," Martin exclaims. "I ain't crazy."

Linda is aware of his history, but "she knows me, the better me." The pair has a meaningful friendship. Martin says they are so close they finish each other's sentences.

Martin also reconnected and repaired things with three of his children, and Martin has 12 grandkids.

I met Martin on Christmas Eve 2013. I had heard people talk highly about the Adam Center and thought working with a mentor—someone whom I could bounce questions off and who might provide some guidance—might be beneficial to me. I am fortunate to have been matched with Martin.

He revealed at our first meeting that he'd been addicted to crack. Though surprised, I appreciated his honesty and sensed Martin would be more relatable than someone who had never faced significant obstacles in life. His transparency made it easier to put my guard down.

Martin and I get together every week or two in a small conference room at the Adam Center. He often shows up sharply dressed in a suit, yet wearing slippers to reduce the ache of gout in his feet. Though he's nearly twice my age, Martin calls me "Brother Keith."

When I ask for advice, Martin offers advice. If I need to talk, he listens. All the while, he encourages me. Sometimes he calls me just to make sure I'm OK.

Despite the many challenges we have faced in our lives, we are both doing our best. We speak openly, often emotionally. We commonly tear up while talking, which I like—I can see his big heart, his empathy for another human being. Because of this, Martin and I have a strong bond. He is like the African-American uncle I never had!

At the end of February 2014, I asked Martin if he'd be willing to be included in this book. Martin agreed to think about the idea, pointing out that we came into each other's lives for a reason. As usual, he switched the conversation back to me, saying he believes God has a plan for me.

The following week, Martin said he would love to be a part of the project, which would be worthwhile if just one person were reached. Happy and relieved, I mentioned I could alter his name in order to protect him or his family. Without hesitation, Martin responded: "No. Why hide?"

We stood up to hug, both misty-eyed. Martin said he loved me and I told Martin I loved him, too. I thanked him for his willingness to tell his story, but Martin corrected, "*Our* story."

Again, he quickly took the focus off himself: "You are seeking, Brother Keith, and you will get there. God has great things in store for you." Then Martin prayed the book would aid others who are struggling.

Martin is happiest when a person accepts God into his or her life. He loves seeing a "converted soul," one who has risen above hurdles. When this happens, Martin realizes he has something new in common with them.

Martin not only overcame a great deal in his personal life, he now uses his trials to set a positive example and to assist others. Former party friends see him walking into church with a Bible under his arm these days. Witnessing Martin's transformation with their own eyes, some ask him what happened and how they can have the same results. Martin tells them his turnaround is all about Jesus. To date, five of these once-lost individuals are now clean and seeking God.

Martin continues to live his life with joy and hopes I'll meet a special young woman and invite him to my wedding.

"I'm trying to hold on, even if I have to come in a wheel-chair," he says. I replied I would try to hurry up. Martin became a great-grandfather in May 2015 and was so excited that he made me promise to include this news in the book.

I have the utmost respect for Martin. He takes responsibility for his past and refrains from making excuses or blaming anyone else. "It happened. I was curious and did things because I wanted to do them," he says. "Knowing what I know now, would I have done it? No! It started out as pleasure, money, and women, but it was the wrong pleasure."

I don't judge my friend for once being addicted to crack cocaine; I admire him for rising above his demons. Martin still searches for answers and wants redemption. His main advice is to trust in God, no matter what the circumstances.

Martin is living proof people can change for the better and make a difference.

....

If you would like to make a donation in honor of Martin, please do so at American Cancer Society (www.cancer.org).

Beth

September 7, 2010, seemed like just another beautiful, sunny Tuesday. Beth Fox's son Jack had a good day at preschool, and afterward Beth took Jack and his 2-year-old sister, Allison, to their grandma's house, only 0.2 miles from their own home. (Beth's three older children were still at school.) Ordinarily, Jack would have to be carried out of his grandmother's kicking and screaming, but on this day he wanted to leave for some reason.

Beth, with glasses over blue eyes, medium-length sandy-blonde hair, and an ever-ready, luminous smile, loaded the van. She realized she had left behind some strawberries, so Jack and his younger sister headed toward the back yard to retrieve them. Suddenly and completely out of character, 3-year-old Jack let go of his sister's hand, changed directions, and took off down the driveway. Though Jack visited his grandma's house nearly every day, he'd never made a dash for the street before. "So many weird things happened that day," Beth recalls.

When she looked up and saw Jack running toward traffic, Beth yelled for him to stop, but he didn't. A vehicle driven by a woman texting on her cell phone struck Jack. In a matter of seconds, his short life was over. (The driver drove off, but was later caught.) A distracted driver had killed Beth's only son before his fourth birthday.

Beth says:

"Jack was our energetic, never-stopping, fearless little boy. He was all boy through and through. There wasn't anything he wouldn't try or anything he didn't think he could do. Determination and will power were very abundant in Jack. He loved to run. Running as fast as he could was one of his favorite things to do. He was always running or playing with his sisters.

"He was very protective of his little sister. They both thought the world of each other. And Jack's three older sisters thought the world of both of them as well. He was such a funny kid. Jack had a smile and a personality that were contagious. Plus, the sparkle in his eyes just lit up the room when he entered. You couldn't help but to fall in love with him. He had such a bright future."

Beth has played the scene over in her head every day. She has to live the rest of her life with that guilt, and she doesn't think she will ever get over losing her son.

Beth continues: "It was horrible. I wouldn't wish that on anyone. I looked away for a second. Everyone looks away for a second, but that is what happened in my second."

She could have taken the easy way out. Many in her position would have numbed the pain with drugs, medication, or alcohol; still others might have ended their lives.

Despite her guilt and devastation, Beth turned her focus from Jack's tragedy to her other children. "I still have four girls that need me," she says.

Astonishingly, Beth holds no resentment for the woman who took her son's life:

"I have no anger. It was an accident. It's not like she set out that day…I'm angry at what happened, not at her. She didn't do it on purpose. I never saw the point of being angry. It won't change anything. It won't bring him back."

Before Jack's passing, Beth had everything she wanted. She had gone to travel school and became a flight attendant. She married a pilot in 1996 and they had five kids. Then the rug was pulled out from beneath them.

"You finally get to your goal, a house and kids, and think your life is set," says Beth. "Then…wow. This was not in my plans."

She and her husband handled the heartbreak much differently. Unlike her husband, Beth saw the incident happen right in front of her. Looking back, Beth says their ways of dealing with their son's death weren't something they could change. The couple divorced in 2014, three and a half years after the tragedy.

Dealing with a divorce—with four kids to consider—on top of grieving for her son has been tough. Beth describes these past few years as "a whirlwind tour that totally turned everything upside down."

After the divorce, she was left mostly on her own without much emotional support. Well-intentioned people wanted to help, but no one knew what to do. Even her closest friends didn't know what to say or how to deal with her.

After 14 years of being a stay-at-home mom, Beth had to go back to work. She acknowledges that balancing work and kids was a big change. Fortunately, rejoining the work force turned out to be a blessing in many ways.

Initially, Beth worked as a bank teller. The bank did mainly commercial transactions and had few walk-in customers, leaving her bored and unfulfilled. Her friend Raneé, whose kids went to preschool with Beth's, banked there. Sensing Beth's frustration and need for stimulation from her job, Raneé asked Beth one day, "How do you do it?"

Soon thereafter, Raneé called her about an opening at Rafey Chiropractic. The concept at Rafey resonated with Beth, who eagerly accepted the position of handling insurance and financing for Dr. Jennifer. Though her pay would be lower than at the bank, working at an office with a mission she supports concerned Beth more.

"People come into your life for a reason," Beth affirms. "I found a job that was perfect for me when I needed it."

She fell in love with the position and the staff quickly. Beth values that the women at Rafey are independent but genuinely care for one another and for the patients. The staff has a strong bond and is like a family.

Beth tells a story about her coworker demonstrating this special connection. After working together for several months, her coworker couldn't keep silent any longer—she'd been praying for Beth from the time of Jack's fatality, long before she even knew Beth. And now life had them working side by side.

Beth is grateful for her current career:

"I have to work now, so I want to make a difference while I'm doing it, especially since much of life is spent at work. I love what I do. I love Dr. Jennifer and all the girls that work there. It's so family-oriented.

"I like waking up and looking forward to going to work. I have a passion for my job and working with people, so I want to put my all into it. When I'm at work, I'm away from my kids, so I want my job to be something I believe in."

September 7, 2015, marked the five-year anniversary of Jack's passing, though it seems like just yesterday to Beth. She recently had talked to a woman who lost a child 20 years ago. The woman told her the hole never goes away, but time helps you learn how to live with the void.

Beth still has awful days. Something seemingly small will bring back the memories and sting, leaving her a mess. "People who don't know my situation might think I'm crazy," she says, shrugging. "That is why I will never judge someone else, because I don't know what they're going through."

After the accident, Beth took her girls to a program where they interacted with other children who had lost siblings. Her kids benefitted from the experience and Beth now wants to find time to volunteer in this type of setting, drawing on her first-hand knowledge of loss and the grieving process.

She knows the hurt all too well and wants to help others facing that type of heartache.

Beth has felt for a while that she is meant to do something along these lines. Her first step was setting up a foundation in her son's memory, "Jack's Forever 3 Foundation" (jacksforever3.com):

> Jack's death is a parent's worst nightmare that we hope never happens to anyone. However, the three years we had with him were a true blessing that we will always treasure.
>
> Since September 7th, 2010, our family has made it our mission to promote driver awareness so that we can try to keep a tragedy like ours from happening to another family. We realized the great need to educate drivers on the importance of staying aware at all times and the potential consequences that can occur from being distracted.

Jack's Forever 3 Foundation strives "to take our tragedy and turn it into something positive in our community." In addition to encouraging attentive driving, the foundation raises money for needy kids in Beth's community. "We want to surprise families that don't have the means to do anything 'extra' by giving them a 'Simple Blessing' to help put a smile on a child's face the way Jack put a smile on so many faces."

On September 10, 2016, the sixth annual "Jack's Forever 3 'Still Running' 5k Run/Walk" was scheduled to take place.

(Running was Jack's favorite thing to do.) To date, Beth has raised approximately $55,000.

Beth hopes to visit schools to warn of the dangers of distracted driving, caused by texting, putting on make-up, etc. Drivers think looking away from the road for a second is OK, but that second can make the difference. "People think that nothing bad can happen to them, but look what happened to me and her," Beth reminds.

(I found this statement telling of Beth's character. The "and her" refers to the woman who hit Jack. Without even thinking, Beth lumps the two of them together as people dealing with a terrible event. She's not hateful or accusatory whatsoever. When I asked Beth what kind of punishment the woman received, Beth said she thinks six months in jail and four and a half years of probation, but she's not sure. Someone more bitter than Beth would know exactly how long the sentence lasted. Beth's empathy and ability to forgive awe me.)

Jack's death changed Beth's perspective on things. Beth realized she isn't in control. Much more relaxed now, she no longer plans everything down to the minute detail. "If the kids have clothes that are clean and fit, we're good," Beth laughs. "They don't have to match perfectly."

Though she believes she will never be fully happy again since her son was taken, she strives to stay positive. "The only thing I have control of is me—my choices and what I say and do," she says. Nonetheless, Beth describes the struggle with her guilt as a constant battle.

Her girls are 16, 14, 12, and 8. All four play soccer year-round, and the two middle girls are into basketball and archery. They get along well for the most part and take care of one another. Beth endeavors to keep open communication with her kids so they know they can come to her about anything.

They, too, have grown from Jack's untimely passing. Beth explains:

"They are more aware of loss and appreciate things a lot more. They are much more compassionate and caring because of it. I hate that they had to learn that so young. They're great qualities to have, which is good. I just hate how they got them."

A story exemplifies this compassion beyond their years. Not long ago, a janitor at one of the girls' schools lost a son in a car accident. Completely on her own, Beth's daughter made a sympathy card for the janitor. She knew what losing a loved one felt like and wanted to ease the suffering of someone else.

Beth has been working to promote driver awareness through a partnership between her foundation and local police departments. She's been able to buy a simulator that shows teenagers what can happen when they are distracted behind the wheel, and now Beth and members of law enforcement soon will be visiting schools, fairs, and driver's education classes. Even though she works and has four kids, Beth hopes to be present at events as often as she can.

After her son died, Beth wanted to donate to organizations teaching youngsters driving safety, but she found none. So, as is her personality, she chose the tougher route and decided to start a program herself. Beth is excited her dream is getting nearer. She says, "I feel like I'm that close to what I've wanted for the last several years." She hopes the joint venture is successful and spreads widely.

At Jack's funeral service, the minister talked about there being two paths to take when confronted with a major obstacle. There is the easy way, which often includes taking drugs or drinking excessively in an effort to avoid the pain. But there is also the difficult course, which involves facing the hurt by getting out of bed every day and making every effort to go on with life.

The minister's message sank in for Beth. She chose the hard path. Beth not only wakes up to confront every day—including the unending questions and sadness—but also does her best to be a great mother and to help others at her job and through the foundation honoring her son.

....

If you would like to make a donation in honor of Beth Fox and/or in memoriam of her son, Jack Carpenter, please do so at "Jack's Forever 3 Foundation" (jacksforever3.com).

Curt (part two)

In *Escape with One's Life: Learning to Live with Survival*—his book detailing his brush with death and efforts to heal physically and emotionally—Curt Schaeffer points out he grew up near the home of the Wright Brothers in Dayton, Ohio. In fact, the hill adjacent to the aerial pioneers' former home was his favorite sled-riding spot as a youth. That Curt was raised in the birthplace of aviation is quite ironic.

His father, Brad, was a "conservative attorney with a strong sense of ethics," and his mother, Paula, "took on one crusade after another—civil rights, the Vietnam War, and spiritual development." Curt's maternal grandparents worked a productive gold mine in a small Ecuadorian village in the 1920s, which instilled a desire in Curt to learn Spanish from a young age. Curt attributes his sense of adventure and independent character to his mother and her "frontier-like upbringing."

A sociology major at Pitzer College in Claremont, California, Curt "found more practical education outside the classroom" as an AmeriCorps VISTA volunteer (like the Peace Corps, but within the United States) at a mental health center and as a resource coordinator in a prison:

> My motivation to work with other people came
> from my extroverted nature and a genuine interest

in making my little piece of the world a better place. I liked people, liked being involved with people and groups and pursuing a career in the helping professions was attractive. I was a child of the '60s. Making money and accumulating material possessions were not on my mind. Following my interests and forsaking conventional career paths guided my decisions.

After graduation, Curt worked with young offenders at a public defender's office in Portland, Oregon. The job was interesting, but he found himself somewhat burned out after two years. He'd saved enough money to pursue his lifelong dream of traveling for six months around Latin America, a land he'd heard much about.

"Once I passed into a new world of different sights, sounds, smells, and language, I was hooked," he recalls. "I was lonely and scared at times, but always challenged by the newness of it all."

Curt felt he belonged in Latin America. He landed a teaching job at an international school in Cochabamba, Bolivia, where he stayed for two years. He then returned to the United States to get a master's degree in international administration at the School for International Training in Vermont, his "foot in the door to working overseas." For the next five years, Curt worked various management jobs in Peru and Bolivia with the U.S. government and international nonprofit organizations.

As with his wanderlust, Curt's desire to do humanitarian work seems to be hereditary. Years ago, my uncle (and godfather), Roger, attended St. Paul's Episcopal Church with the Schaeffer family. Curt's parents and their four boys lived next door to the church. Paula, Curt's mother, was Roger's Sunday school teacher. When Roger was in the second grade, his mother died of breast cancer, so his father sought out a family to act as godparents for him.

Paula and Brad Schaeffer stepped up. Roger reflects: "They were so welcoming and took me into their family. They were a source of stability and guidance."

Unfortunately, Roger's father passed away during Roger's senior year of high school. When Roger went away to college, he'd stay with the Schaeffers during the summers. "I fell into a truly unique, happy, and fortunate circumstance," Roger remembers. "They had the resources to take me in and were not afraid to challenge me."

Roger describes Paula as bright and open-minded. Like the four Schaeffer boys, Roger was encouraged to explore the world around him and not be simply a "normal" person. Roger also learned to be responsible for his actions. For all of this, he still feels lucky: "I had four brothers, and the relationships have grown over time. The Schaeffers have adventurous spirits…and know how to have a good time."

By his own admission, Curt has always been "offbeat" and opinionated. His past CARE colleague and later American Association of Retired Persons (AARP) president and CEO

William D. Novelli states in the preface to Curt's book, "Even among CARE's many interesting and unique people, Curt stood out." Mr. Novelli describes him as carefree, but also hardworking and well-respected in his time with CARE. Roger adds, "Curt is very, very intelligent, warm, engaging, caring, and has a keen and wry sense of humor."

While in Central America, Curt fell in love with a Venezuelan woman, Magaly Quintero Marquez, and the two married in 1985. They spent their first three years of marriage in La Paz, Bolivia—Curt overseeing a health care project and Magaly an office manager for the World Health Organization. In 1988, they moved to New York, where Curt worked for CARE as the Deputy Regional Manager for Latin American Operations.

Then the Schaeffers' lives were changed forever.

Curt's commercial air flight from San Jose, Costa Rica, to Tegucigalpa, Honduras, collided with a mountainside on October 21, 1989. Due to the thick clouds (as well as pilot negligence—more on this later), the pilots were flying closer to land than they realized and clipped the side of the mountain at Cerro de Hula. Both the captain and first officer survived, relatively unscathed, along with 13 others. The plane exploded an estimated five to 10 minutes later, and then everything went eerily silent until emergency personnel rushed to the scene.

October 21 in Honduras is Armed Forces Day, so mainly students and interns were present at the hospital where Curt, one of the 15 survivors, was taken. The facility was woefully unprepared for this type of strain even on a normal day, but especially on a national holiday. Confusion reigned and important steps were missed. To make matters worse, the airline initially reported there were no survivors. (From his years living in Central America, Curt knew the people were used to being told inaccurate information, often blatant lies, and had a justified mistrust of authorities.)

Luckily for Curt, some of his CARE colleagues had heard the news even before the family members of those on board Flight 414. About an hour after he reached the hospital, a few friendly faces located him with considerable effort and were by his side to offer encouragement. Delighted to find Curt alert, even joking around, the CARE team sprang into action to aid him in this ultimate time of need.

He told them several times, perhaps to convince himself: "I am alive. I am alive." Only when a doctor told him how few passengers had survived did Curt begin to comprehend the devastation—and his luck. But Curt's chief concern was his wife.

Magaly was waiting to board a flight to meet Curt in Honduras when a fellow traveler told her an aircraft had gone down in Tegucigalpa. Magaly checked at the counter and was astounded to learn the plane was Curt's:

"I knew for sure now that Curt was on the plane that crashed. I did not react. I could not believe it. I did not move. I started to cry, but at the same time I tried to control myself and think what I could do. I was alone and my flight to Tegucigalpa was due to start boarding in 10 minutes. I thought about calling Curt's parents but decided it was not a good idea, since it was tragic news and I didn't know anything more. I was so nervous and afraid about the whole situation that I did not know where to go or what to do."

She boarded for a three-hour trip to Tegucigalpa, unsure if her husband was alive. Halfway through, Curt explains, Magaly "had a sudden rush of adrenaline…a special feeling, like an internal message telling her that I was all right." Magaly asked an attendant for information on the accident and was told a handful had survived.

Just before landing in Tegucigalpa, Magaly found out her husband was one of the few. "I could not believe it," she said. "After torturing myself for hours, now I was crying out of happiness!"

CARE staff met Magaly at the airport and assured her Curt was OK. Priority No. 1 was moving him to a better facility for urgent care and then transporting him to the United States as briskly as possible. The day was chaotic, but knowing he was in the capable hands of the CARE staff kept Curt calm. He knew they would take care of him.

Thanks to his crack team, Curt was taken to a private clinic and wrapped head to toe to cover his burns. A medevac doctor noticed something was amiss and, consulting an X-ray, confirmed Curt had a collapsed right lung. The doctor removed air and fluid to re-inflate the lung, causing Curt tremendous distress. The procedure was vital. He wouldn't have lived more than three to four more hours with the damaged lung, considering his burns and prior state of shock.

Curt was given the green light to fly and was driven to the airport by ambulance. Upon arrival, he was reunited with his anxious wife. Magaly had been led to believe Curt was in great shape and later confessed that his true condition took her aback.

Curt believes everyone who got him on the Learjet to Miami, Florida, "had been sent by some higher authority to take care of me and see me safely out of the country." He adds, "They accomplished the near impossible."

Exhausted, Curt slept much of the way to Miami. Magaly sat by his feet and medical personnel monitored his vitals. He was taken to Jackson Memorial in downtown Miami, a hospital with an excellent burn unit.

Twenty-five percent of his body had sustained second- and third-degree burns, including his face, ears, chest, arms, hands, and lower legs. Burn treatment, Curt explains, is delicate, complicated, and expensive, involving "a high-protein diet, daily physical therapy, timely removal of dead skin, and plenty of rest." Due to the constant threat of infection, visitors were limited, any items from outside were strictly regulated, and unconsumed food was swiftly discarded. But with diligence, the rehab process itself can be somewhat rapid.

Curt was kept on a respirator in the intensive care unit the first few days. In retrospect, Curt didn't know the extent of his burns and how grueling the recovery process would be.

Having Magaly and his brother Alan by his side in Miami made the ordeal somewhat easier. (Fortuitously, Alan was on a fishing trip in the Florida Everglades when he got the news and was waiting for Curt and Magaly when they got to the hospital.)

Curt describes his mindset at the time:

> Immediately after the crash, whatever negative feelings I harbored for the pilots or the airline were secondary to my own physical and psychological recovery. There was no time or energy for hatred or revenge, even though both lingered in the back of my mind. I was a burned and broken individual, and my future was unclear. I had come face to face with my mortality and somehow survived in the face of enormous odds against me. What did this mean? How was I to deal with survival when so many had perished? What was I supposed to do with my survival? These and other questions plagued me and would continue to plague me for years. The immediate concern, though, was my physical recovery.

At the time of the accident, Curt was 39 years old and in good shape. Despite his uncertain state, he was determined to get healthy enough to play his beloved tennis and basketball again. But, he adds, "I had no idea what this would involve."

After three days in the ICU, Curt was moved to the burn unit. Each day began with what Curt called the "Chamber of Horrors," a room where nurses tried to remove as much dead tissue as possible in order to make way for new tissue to grow. The process was pure agony, a fragile balance of making progress without inflicting unbearable pain. Patients were given morphine, but merely a small dose in order to keep them lucid and to prevent possible addiction.

Post-session, a nurse applied cream to prevent contamination—a practice Curt came to love—and then bandaged him with new dressings. Each night, the process was repeated. The nurses dutifully rebuffed his requests for additional morphine. Though they put him through hell, Curt came to see the nurses as angels trying to get their charges better as soon as possible.

Though not as dreadful as the dead skin removal, daily physical therapy was incredibly taxing, yet essential. "I found myself crying from the anguish of moving body parts that had been rendered temporarily non-functional," Curt acknowledges. "I knew I had to do it if I wanted to progress and get out of there."

Surprised to find how emotional he became, Curt often sobbed to the nurses while they worked with him. He was angry at the airline and frustrated with his present condition. He also felt guilt over surviving and was deeply saddened by those killed—"Why me? This is not fair!"

"I was used to being in control of most everything I did, but this was unchartered territory," he says. "I not only didn't like it, but I was scared." Curt worked on his physical recovery diligently but largely disregarded his emotional health.

Fortunately, unlike most of the patients, Curt had family there for support. Magaly was by his side tirelessly. His parents came in from Oregon and his brother Mike came to Miami also. Friends and colleagues visited; cards and phone calls were commonplace. The overwhelming support was flattering and greatly appreciated. Cards included messages such, "I know you like attention, but this is going overboard," and, "There are easier ways to make national news."

The media wanted to interview Curt when he arrived in Miami. Magaly and the hospital staff worried about a horde of reporters in the ICU, for both sanitary concerns and to protect Curt's mental and physical states at an unstable time. Curt replied: "Honey, this is my one chance to be famous. Let them in!" Both local and national media, including CNN, wanted to talk to Curt, but just one reporter and camera crew was permitted, so he chose a local team. He spoke about the impact not only on him, but also on the sizeable Nicaraguan community in Miami.

Curt believes keeping his sense of humor sharp played a significant role in his healing. He enjoyed sneaking a recording of laughter into the nurses' lounge to be heard throughout the unit. This gag seemed to lighten moods every time:

"Burn victims do not move around a lot even though it is a recommended part of their rehabilitation to get out of bed and walk around—assisted or unassisted, depending on the location and severity of the burns. I simply slipped the recorder into the lounge on one of my many walks up and down the main hallway. At the same time, I would turn the laughter tape on and then continue my walk giving me the opportunity to watch the other patients go to the doors of the rooms with smiles on their faces looking for the origin of the laughter."

Removing the dead skin took about two long weeks, a huge relief to Curt. His physical recovery then took off. Witnessing skin re-grow on his body was awe-inspiring. His mindset soared, especially when his doctor cleared him to leave the hospital after nearly a month.

"I could not have asked for a more supportive, nurturing environment to recover in," he says. "CARE paid for all of my treatment expenses, and I really had nothing to worry about except my recovery."

His brother Doug flew in from California to drive him to their parents' home in Ohio, where Curt would continue to recover. (Understandably, Curt wasn't ready to fly.) Curt developed a daily routine to clean and dress his own wounds. He was in a familiar environment, surrounded by loved ones. Magaly continued to work in New York during the week and flew to Ohio every weekend.

Curt recollects, "My month in Dayton was focused on closing the physical wounds and beginning to address my psychological state." Curt saw a therapist, which helped him vent his bottled-up emotions. Nightmares, typically about fires, disrupted his sleep many nights.

Curt returned to New York to start an intensive physical therapy program at the Cornell Medical Center in Manhattan. The demanding, twice-daily exercises focused on building strength in his hands, fingers, and wrists. A tight, elastic full-body suit protected his healing skin "neck to ankles," a cumbersome hindrance worn 24 hours a day for almost two years.

Curt returned to CARE after just two and a half months. CARE offered Curt full disability for a year, but he was "intent on not losing any professional momentum." Throwing himself into his career allowed him to avoid the mental fallout over his near death—staying busy with work kept his mind off his feelings. He saw the accident as a "trophy," enjoying the attention and sympathy, but otherwise acted like nothing happened.

Around a year later, Dr. Susan Shapiro, his psychologist, had misgivings. From her notes:

> On the surface CS has made a remarkable adjustment—almost too good to be true, and that is in part what concerns me. C's ability to get it and keep it "together" has enabled him to go back to work quite quickly and show little evidence to the world at large of the trauma he has been through. He still cannot assimilate what he went through and uses denial to cope with the extent of the trauma.

Curt later looked back with some regret:

> What I lost by going back to work so quickly was an opportunity to engage in my own form of grieving over a trauma that I did not understand and that left me feeling guilty for having survived. I was horrified when a friend living in Honduras sent me the official list of deceased passengers. It seemed to go on endlessly. None of the names were familiar to me, but upon leaving Managua, we were all together on that plane. Thirty minutes later, a handful of us had survived.

Despite the façade, Curt was barely hanging on. Flashbacks tormented him regularly, often during work meetings. He was reliving the catastrophe—known as post-traumatic stress disorder (PTSD)—and occasionally ducked out of meetings to collect himself. Against his psychologist's advice, he chose to swallow his emotions, especially at the office, fearing he would be seen as weak.

Another worry, justifiably, was getting back on an airplane. Because his job required repeated travel, Curt knew he'd have to overcome his fear as soon as possible. After several trips to the airport to watch planes taking off and landing, he faced his fear on a two-hour flight from Dayton to New York one nasty December morning, Magaly by his side.

The trip—the most turbulent he'd ever endured—assured Curt he could handle any flight:

> I have been asked many times since the crash if I am afraid of flying. I made a point of getting back on a plane within months of my mishap and remain a frequent flyer to this day. Each time I step on a plane, my emotional side tells me it may be my last flight, but my rational side says the odds of being involved in another air crash are slim to none. There is always an underlying discomfort during a flight.

After Flight 414, Curt figured there must be a reason why he was one of the few survivors. Perhaps he was destined to do something great for the world. Yet he continued to struggle with survivor's guilt, questioning his fortune when many lost their lives, particularly children.

Curt wrestled with what to do with his life to justify his being alive, until he finally realized what he'd been doing all along—serving others—was enough. He was doing what he could to better the world in his own way. No longer having to validate his continued existence lifted a huge weight off Curt.

Dr. Shapiro prodded him to confront his emotions by returning to Cerro de Hula. Curt and Magaly returned to Honduras a year after the incident. It was not easy to revisit the country, much less the scene of the crash.

Curt walked to the area where he came to in the field. Taken aback to find wreckage still at the site, he knelt beside it and cried uncontrollably. Sadness turned to anger.

He descended to the dirt road where he'd gotten in the back of the truck on that fateful day. Gazing at the mountainside where people had lost their lives just a year before, Magaly hugged Curt while he wept before they departed. Over the next week, he personally thanked the CARE staff members who got him to Miami promptly.

On the way home, Curt and his wife stopped at the hospital in Miami to thank the nurses in the burn unit. He was pleased to find that they didn't recognize him now that his burns had healed. Seeing one of their success stories elated the staff.

The tragedy and Curt's recovery meant Magaly had taken a backseat. "Everyone wanted to hear about my experience, while Magaly was often left in the background," Curt concedes. "I was so focused on my own needs that I was not even aware that she was having a tough time." Magaly eventually sought her own counseling. The couple would debrief after each of their sessions, which improved their communication.

PTSD can destroy relationships, but Curt and Magaly grew closer and appreciated each other more from the tribulation. While Curt is grateful for the support from family and friends and for the counseling he received, he says he might not have made it through without his wife's unwavering love and devotion:

"Magaly's incredible support throughout this long period of rehabilitation and recovery was a big reason for my returning to a normal life. Her most valuable help came in just being present with me. This means that she consistently made herself available to me. Whether I needed her or not, I knew that she was always by my side—assisting, guiding, and loving."

On March 24, 1992, they were blessed with a baby girl. The Schaeffers were now a family, with Alexa being the main focus. Beaming, Curt says, "The birth of my daughter was truly the greatest gift I have received in my new life, after my own survival."

Magaly stayed home from work for the first three months. She and Curt made a pact that one of them would raise Alexa. Curt says, "The thought of handing our daughter over to a stranger and giving that person primary responsibility for raising her was unacceptable to both of us." When Magaly accepted a position with International Planned Parenthood Federation, Curt took a leave of absence from CARE to raise his daughter, his "most satisfying career move."

Being a stay-at-home father at that time was even less common than nowadays. Their resolution somewhat flabbergasted several family members, friends, and coworkers. His prior colleague, William D. Novelli, respected Curt's decision. "Curt was just a different kind of guy," he says.

Curt's time with his daughter was rewarding, but he quickly found caring for an infant was far more arduous than office work. With hindsight, he knows much of the difficulty had less to do with diapers and more to do with his ego. Within the first week, Curt realized his job title and salary were more important to him than he'd thought.

He returned to CARE after 11 months and the Schaeffers relocated from New York to Atlanta when CARE moved its offices there. Curt continued working with CARE until May 1998, eventually rising to Chief of Staff, but he was restless toward the end. He couldn't pinpoint the cause, but he felt cooped up in an office setting. Curt sensed a change was necessary—his trauma needed to be dealt with.

Outwardly, he was composed; inwardly, Curt was frustrated and confused. He still needed to grieve and heal. When he finally decided to leave the organization, Curt's main motivation was to write a book about his survival:

"Nine years after the crash I still had too many unanswered questions, nightmares and unsettled feelings. Years of therapy helped, but I was driven to do something on my own. I had to act."

Initially, Curt wanted merely to document his trials. Then he felt compelled to seek out the other survivors to conduct interviews for a book detailing the calamity and its effect on his life and on the lives of the other survivors and the families of the deceased. Over the next five years, Curt took consulting jobs to pay the bills while he worked on his story.

He took a number of trips to Central America to interview people affected by the catastrophe. He attended the anniversary Mass at Cerro de Hula for several years. (The site is now a park with a beautiful monument honoring the deceased passengers.)

Curt is thankful for the "personal catharsis" from writing *Escape with One's Life: Learning to Live with Survival* and for interacting with others influenced by the accident. Many of his questions were answered and he could let go of his hatred toward those responsible for the plane crash. Writing his book was key to the process.

"Confronting this experience after nine years brought me face to face with my long dormant fears, frustration and anger over what had happened and how it had affected me," he says. "My journey became a personal pursuit that forced me to examine my own healing along with others who had experienced painful survival or catastrophic loss."

I won't go into depth about the other passengers—Curt already did this quite well. (I hope you will read his riveting, first-person account for yourself. There is much more to his book than what I cover, including descriptions of the ordeal told by other survivors, the heroic actions of passengers and Curt's colleagues at CARE, and almost surreal accounts of people who for various reasons were not on Flight 414 after planning to be originally. His book is available in paperback and eBook on Amazon.com in both English and Spanish. I interviewed Curt a few times recently, and although I use direct quotes from his book, my account is based on his responses years after his book's publication.)

I will mention that Curt found the methods of healing among the survivors to be varied. Some relied on strong religious faiths, others on family. Several continued on with a new purpose to help others.

Nearly all whom Curt interviewed expressed gratitude for being alive, but also acknowledged that the upsetting memories probably never would go away. The littlest thing would bring them right back to the horrors of that mountainside, to sights and sounds they'd never forget. To their credit, though, Curt says: "I was struck by the fact that the survivors I met and talked with did not waste time blaming the pilots or the airline for what happened. They recognized their good fortune and appeared to be a collectively positive group, intent on looking ahead and not back."

Some of the loved ones of the deceased were less forgiving and attempted to take the pilots to task. A month after Flight 414 went down, the captain and first officer were indicted for homicide. Curt says: "The pilots were criminally charged in Honduras but were found not guilty by a panel of three judges in a 2-1 vote. The airline was held accountable in a class action (civil suit) in Houston, Texas, so there is documented culpability, but it never directly affected the pilots even though their negligence is clear." Despite discovering reports had been tampered with, they and the airline were cleared of any wrongdoing.

Curt points out the decision, apparently based on falsified information, was made with unheard-of speed, especially considering the number of lives lost. The first officer even confessed awareness that the aircraft was flying too low but did not speak up out of fear of defying the captain. He also testified to knowing the plane would impact four minutes before it did.

On top of everything else, an investigation established the aircraft's ground proximity warning system (GPWS) wasn't working. In fact, the warning system had not been used for several flights—the pilots were disarming the GPWS to keep from having to hear the alarm sound when they were too close to land, which would have given them more time to pull up. Nonetheless, no one was faulted for the disaster.

Apparently, neither the captain nor first officer ever flew again. The captain maintained he didn't remember anything from the crash. He now lives a reclusive life. Curt came to believe the pilots "were not evil men, but they committed an evil act."

A local Honduran newspaper interviewed Curt during a visit in 2001. Though his intent wasn't to condemn the captain and first officer, he didn't hold back. "The Pilots are Guilty!" [in Spanish] was the headline the next morning. The pronouncement surprised Curt but "was a measure of retribution, in a way." He says, "There it was for all to see in black and white."

Realizing he'd been hung up on having someone to blame took Curt a long time. He even looked for the pilots a few times on his visits to Central America but was unable to meet them in person. Curt believes they, too, have suffered; life has been rough for them since October 21, 1989. After years of wanting to point an accusing finger, he now sees worrying about them as a waste of time.

He finally redirected the misused energy from focusing on his bitterness toward the captain and first officer to the positives in his life. Curt became more appreciative of his wife and daughter, his family, and his friends. He will never understand why the tragedy happened, but he is grateful to be alive.

"My process of struggling to understand and let go of my inner conflicts started the day of the crash and took 13 years to run its course," he admits. For a while, Curt lived a double life of the jubilant, brave survivor and the furious, yet vulnerable victim. Only after he began his writing project did the latter come out.

Readers have applauded Curt for his honest portrayal. Frequently, he's been told his openness "gave them permission to confront and deal with their own traumas that they had buried years ago." They learned from Curt's example and found the courage to tackle their own issues.

His book put him in touch with people Curt believes went through more than he did—survivors with even more complex rehabilitations or those who lost loved ones. He now can better relate to the struggles of others. Curt has gained compassion; he has gained friends.

The book and subsequent promotion were significant to his healing process. Curt has learned that the more trauma is confronted instead of ignored, the better. Sharing his story with others forced him to deal with his demons continually.

Curt Schaeffer is back to playing tennis and basketball. After many years on the sidelines, he intends to stay active for as long as possible. At one time, Curt was hell-bent on meeting the captain of Flight 414, but more than a quarter century after the tragedy he says, "It's clear that the captain and his family are in some form of purgatory and don't need me to make it worse for them." Curt keeps in touch with some of the crash survivors through occasional notes and Christmas cards, but the group has chosen to go on with their separate lives for the most part.

That said, Curt left full-time employment recently and is lending a hand to a non-profit organization run by another survivor to fundraise for a burn unit in Nicaragua. In fact, the proceeds from Curt's book go to the burn unit. He also hopes to focus more on spreading awareness of his book. Not for monetary success, but "because it does seem to benefit readers." Curt is living out what he told me lately— after a life-changing situation like his, "You can draw benefits if you want, but it's up to the individual."

The memories still upset him. Curt still gets tightness in his throat, his voice cracks, tears come to his eyes. But he's OK with that:

"I believe that I became a less ambitious person after the crash. I set my family and my own well-being as priorities and not how much money I made nor how much power I wielded. I came to the conclusion that my ultimate goal in life was to make a difference in my little community and enjoy myself doing it. After all that I had been through, it really was a simple conclusion to reach…

"I find myself approaching the end of the journey. After discussing the crash and its impact with so many people over the years, I find myself talked out and suddenly, losing passion for the subject. I have experienced a breakthrough, a relieving myself of the burden of grief and survivor guilt over the deaths of so many…

"Magaly helped me realize that survival is a rare and precious gift. It was finally time to let go of my bitterness and angst over what had happened and enjoy the gift by focusing on myself and my family. It was time to rid myself of the shadow…

"For whatever reason, I survived a catastrophic plane crash with my physical and mental health largely intact. I would not recommend this experience to anyone, but in many ways it was the best thing that ever happened to me. I am thankful every day for being on this earth."

In *Escape with One's Life*, Curt quotes Viktor Frankl: "What is to give light must endure burning." Curt Schaeffer has endured burning, literally and figuratively, and was able to recover the light inside him that has always wanted to serve others.

If you would like to make a donation in honor of Curt Schaeffer or in memory of any of those lost on Flight 414, please do so at The Burned Children Care Foundation (www.aproquen.org/en/; APROQUEN is the acronym of the foundation's Spanish name), which provides free care to children in Nicaragua suffering from burns.

Acknowledgments

Obviously the biggest thanks go to the people who agreed to open their hearts and lives to me so I could write this book. They had me into their homes and generously shared their stories so others could benefit. I thank all of you from the bottom of my heart. Much love, respect, appreciation, and admiration to all of you.

Sincere gratitude to Raquel Gonzales, Sue Frey, and Father Robert Hater for reading my manuscript and giving me invaluable feedback. I'd also like to thank my mom and dad for helpful edits of the first draft.

I am forever indebted to Lori Highlander and Jennifer Scroggins at KiCam Projects for believing in this book. Lori kindly gave me my first chance and Jennifer's keen eye greatly enhanced my book. I am looking forward to all the good things we are going to do together. Thank you.

Many thanks for assistance from Kelly Myers and the staff at Rafey Chiropractic…Joy's co-graduates from Nica Yoga—Jacq, Cynthia, and Lindsey…Magaly Schaeffer…my uncle, Roger Hommel…and anyone else I might have missed.

Last but not least, sincere thank you to you, dear reader. I hope you enjoyed this book and were inspired in some way. Many thanks and all the best!

About the Author

Keith Maginn was born and raised in Cincinnati, Ohio, the youngest of four children. He attended Miami University in Oxford, Ohio, as an Evans Scholar. After earning his bachelor's degree in sociology, he relocated to Knoxville, Tennessee, to work for AmeriCorps and for Habitat for Humanity. Keith returned to Cincinnati after living nearly 10 years in east Tennessee. He enjoys being surrounded by family and friends.

Though writing is his passion, he also enjoys sports, meditation, yoga, reading, and live music. Keith released *Turning This Thing Around*, an inspiring self-help memoir, in December 2010. In January 2013, he published *Goodwill Tour: Paying It Forward*, detailing a 3,000-mile philanthropic road trip through the southeastern United States. Both books are available in paperback and e-book on Amazon. com or at keithmaginn.com. Keith feels writing to help and inspire others is his life's purpose.